The eight laws for finding
inner fulfilment and wisdom,
unlocking the miracle of true self
and lasting happiness

Baron Benoni Robu

From the author of *How Eating Pigs' Potatoes Almost Made Me a Billionaire* – a new book that will challenge you to become the best version of yourself. Are you ready?

To follow your heart,
Just walk towards the light,
To reach the wildest dreams,
Defeat the doubts and fears.

First published 2024 by
Baron of Dublin Publishing
82A Northway Estate,
Finglas, Dublin 11, D11 R840
Tel: 01 8569431
Email: bengreenbaron@yahoo.ie
Website: www.baronofdublin.ie

ISBN 978-1-99932573-2

Cover design by Design for Writers

Contents

Foreword by Pat Falvey

I crossed paths with the Baron of Dublin, Baron Benoni Robu, back in 2019, during a gathering of the Professional Speaking Association in Dublin. His presence was electric, brimming with passion and a depth of knowledge that seemed to emanate from within. The Baron captivated us with his personal journey, as recounted in his debut book, *How Eating Pigs' Potatoes Almost Made Me a Billionaire*.

However, I couldn't shake the feeling that he had more wisdom to share with fellow travellers on life's winding road. So, I eagerly awaited his next offering.

That wait concluded with the release of From Coal to Diamonds, his latest book. Within its pages lie captivating narratives and profound insights for those seeking answers amidst life's uncertainties – from the peaks of triumph to the valleys of adversity. Embedded within these tales is a new-found understanding of our intrinsic human nature, coupled with a generous call to share and pass on our self-discoveries.

If you find yourself caught between the echoes of the past and the haze of an uncertain future, the Baron's book offers clarity and ignites the spark for your personal odyssey. It may not unfold as you initially anticipate; instead, it reveals a humbler, more authentic perspective on yourself and your journey. Yet beyond this initial revelation lies an exhilarating adventure waiting to unfold.

Through practical counsel and profound insights, the Baron's book possesses the power to revolutionise your life or, at the very least, to open a window into your heart, revealing your untapped potential. Grounded in his own lived experiences, the Baron's philosophy resonates deeply because he practises what he preaches.

In every speck of coal lies the potential for a gleaming diamond. Embrace the process and let your brilliance shine forth!

Introduction

Diamonds among the pigs' potatoes

I collected my daughter from school one day – she must have been about eleven years old. On our way home, she asked me what a doctor, a teacher and an artist earned. I probably mentioned that a doctor made a lot of money because she declared that she would become a doctor. I knew that she loved painting very much and dreamed of becoming an artist. So, I asked her, 'What about your love of painting? Would you just give it up?' My questions caught her unawares, and I could see her becoming confused, not knowing anymore what she really wanted. Two simple direct questions had changed her perspective and forced her to rethink her position. Of course, as an eleven-year-old, she still had plenty of time to make up her mind.

I have learnt from experience that the most difficult questions to answer are the simplest ones, the most direct, the ones that cut to the core of the matter.

So now I ask *you*: How worried are you right now? Is all well with your soul, or are you troubled by thoughts or by something that happened in the past? Do you think your life is hard, or maybe not fair? Is there any burden you carry that you'd like to get rid of? And, if you see yourself in these questions, what are you going to do about it?

If you think your life is a daily struggle, you are not alone. The danger is that when you are in anguish you can forget one simple truth: that your life is precious. Because life – *this* life, *your* life – is truly miraculous. Just think about it. If I didn't tell you to stop and look around, right now, you might continue through your day without thinking. So, stop for a second. Open your eyes. Wake up. Become aware of yourself, right now, as you are sitting with this book. Feel the book in your hand. You have eyes that can see rainbows, clouds and people talking around you; that can read this book. You can be aware of the scent of the ink coming from these pages or taste the salty tears of joy. All these are miraculous in different ways. Take a good look at the person holding the book, at yourself, and say, 'I am life. I am alive. And it feels good.'

If a moment of realisation like this doesn't bring you instant joy, there is a reason for that. What is it? Too many broken dreams in your life? Too many failures? That doesn't mean that you have to carry their burden with you. What if I told you that you can stop all your suffering right now. Today. You can decide to change your life and to believe in yourself. You can stop letting your fears and doubts control you and your future. Are you ready to change? Well, you are here, so all I can say is, so far so good: you passed the first test.

In every human being, there is a dream, a longing for joy, for infinity, for belonging. That desire is built into our DNA. There are also inner struggles and unknown fears, and these are the daily battles we re-enact every single day in our minds. There is also the troublesome feeling that we are more, and that we can do more.

Our life, very much like our world, is in a state of infinite possibilities and endless predicament. So where do we start? The place to start is your mind. Your mind is a wonderful mystery. It sounds complicated, but it is simpler than you think. Your thoughts are more real than you think, and we have the ability to change their very substance. What starts as a little seed, once awakened, grows into an extraordinary awareness with limitless potential. With a bit of effort, we are able to open the window towards the intimate union with the source of creation, preparing for the next level: understanding life, love and beauty. That next level has its foundation in humility and reverence for life. All you have to do is be patient with yourself.

The purpose of this book is to provide you with a map to point you towards the greatest treasure you have ever discovered. Many people who have dared to dream will tell you that at the right time, at the specific crossroad in their lives, the right door opened for them. The same will happen for you. How do I know? I know because I've been there. I've been through what you are going through right now. I have travelled this path, and I know how it feels.

I was born in Communist Romania, under a dictatorship that wanted to crush all that was beautiful and free in a human being. The regime wanted to create 'new people' for the Communist Party, people with no personal dreams and no aspirations. The idea was that the Party would do the thinking and the dreaming for them. And the ruling too. The people would just follow the rules and the leaders and work tirelessly towards an ideal that was all an illusion.

It was during my childhood, under that pressure, that I learnt so much about human nature. I learnt from the people around me, from family, from friends, from those who helped and from those who betrayed. Under a regime that managed to infiltrate everywhere and everything, where brother betrayed brother for a better job or some extra food – even *there* – they could not suppress the dreams and the desire for freedom deep within.

I remember clearly one October day, at the age of ten, I went to buy bread, but there was no bread in the shop. Bread was always in short supply. After a few hours' wrestling and pushing in a queue of adults who seemed to me more like rugby players, I came home empty-handed. Upset, hungry and deeply disappointed, I could not understand the Communist propaganda that we were living in a rich country. The only option left for us was to eat the potatoes from the pigs' trough – 'the pigs' potatoes', the food we fed the pigs. They were sour and grey.

I knew there and then that I did not come into this world only for pigs' potatoes and rock salt. I felt so bitter, and a deep sorrow gripped my heart. I started to cry. It was my birthday; how couldn't I remember! The rain came to my rescue and helped hide the tears, the pain, the hunger and my pride. I wanted to run away and never come back again.

It was in that moment that I made a promise to myself: *This will never happen again.* I knew then that my mission was to break the chain of poverty inherited from previous generations. On that October evening, I planted the seed of a dream, the size of a grain of sand, a light that guided me through the years, always, across the borders of Europe and the loneliness of my inner journey. It was that little seed of faith that kept me going and helped me transform from the darkness of coal into a beautiful shining diamond.

I arrived in Ireland in the autumn of 1997. Living in a free country, as an adult, was a big change for me, and embracing my new life felt very odd at the beginning. Having come from a place where survival and watching my back were daily habits, I had to learn to relax and enjoy my new freedom. It took me years to let go of the old routines.

Long after arriving in the West, I was still accusing the oppressive Communist regime back home for my own failures. By pointing the finger and looking for answers outside me, I was refusing in my stubbornness to learn the lessons masked by the anguish itself. I wasn't ready to acknowledge my responsibility for my own mistakes. It was an easy blame game, even though, deep inside, I knew that all my present decisions were mine and mine alone and had nothing to do with the past.

Why do we like to hang on to the past so much? The past is built by our habits and routines, and the truth is that we become addicted to them. We get so used to one way of living that it becomes our prison. We refuse to move on and to fly free. We forget to dance to the music of life. So remember: before you commit to a new future, you have to free yourself from the heavy, rusty shackles of your past. You will have many questions about it. I'm sure you don't have all the answers right now. You might have no answers at all – and that's totally fine. You will also have doubts and fears. It doesn't mean that your future is lost. You can make a start by imagining a new future. By doing this, you are shaping your future for a new purpose.

Everything all around you is a perception of your mind. In a way, you 'created' the world you are seeing, even though you may still think that on your own you can't do anything to change it. The truth is this: there is much you can do, but it takes courage. Courage means stepping into the unknown, and the unknown means change. Human beings don't like change. But if you find your courage and set yourself on the road of self-inquiry and discovery, believe me, you will never look back.

We can prepare for change by understanding first why we oppose it. The need for change and the fear of change are two opposing instincts within us. Most of the time, fear wins. It is the terror of the unknown that makes us stay in abusive relationships or continue in a soulless job that drains all our energy. We feel we have so much to lose.

It's not that difficult to understand why we are so afraid. When we forget our true self, our dreams, our aspirations, we cover our true identity with something we are not. To rediscover your true identity, you have to peel off the old version of yourself. It's a job only you can do, a decision only you can take. And it paralyses most of us.

At the deepest, purest level, we all want the same thing. We all dream the same dream. How we get there, though, is different, and that is something that only adds to the beauty of this miracle called life. The capacity to transform ourselves is already built in our system, but we choose to bury and disregard this ability. So, instead of being authentic and letting our light shine, we decide to follow others, many times blindly and without asking ourselves, 'Is this the direction I want to go?' Even when things go wrong, instead of listening to our inner voice that tells us to stop and take stock, we continue to chase shadows and to please the crowds. It's little surprise that, in the end, we arrive at the wrong destination and with empty hands. And, as a result, we become more and more isolated.

We live in a connected world, but people feel very much disconnected. We live together, but we are alone. Many people don't remember how it feels to share. To share their time, to share their presence, to be present in the present moment. People feel lost. Our crisis has to do with how we define and explore success. When people say success, it could mean lots of things. How do *you* define success? A new level of understanding life? Running your own business or delivering to your customers the best service or product? Maybe even finding the love of your life?

Success in modern society tends to be measured through a lens where richer, bolder, bigger and faster are, it seems, the only measures of achievement. I have met people whose minds were so deeply rooted in material things that they never had a chance to fully enjoy their accomplishments. Whatever effort they put into acquiring their beautiful mansions, deep down they wondered how they could preserve them, and the thought of losing it all started to creep in. I saw their fear for what the future might bring, and it was paralysing. They seemed to be enjoying life, but they weren't really. Their minds were not in the present moment but thinking frantically ahead.

One client, now also a good friend, told me years ago that he felt trapped, like he was living in a prison. The irony is that he had everything he had ever dreamed of. How did one arrive at this mess, at a point where life felt more like a prison, where one was judge, prisoner and executioner – all three at once? Are we not, all of us, in this position at some point in life? When did we build these barricades around ourselves, these ugly, thick, tall walls? We thought that inside those walls we would feel safe and secure. Do we feel safe now? Not at all.

Unfortunately, the foundations for this elusive security are built on *possessing* instead of *being*, which only leads to isolation and rejection. When we possess, we keep everything for ourselves; we don't share because we feel there's never going to be enough to satisfy our need for safety. That's when that wall around us grows higher. If our neighbour tries to initiate some sort of communication, to build a bridge over our wall, we see it as trespassing. We take it as an offence; we take it personally.

When this compulsiveness for success is pushed to the extreme, it leads to a complete separation of your true self from the rest of the world. In isolation, we forget who we really are and where we come from. Like compulsive marathon runners, competing in complete isolation, the only satisfaction left to us is to grab the shiny gold medal at the end of each race and celebrate in isolation. Not a very optimistic future, is it?

We are caught in this contest to become successful. Even when we sit motionless, we still run our own race inside our heads. Yes, we became more successful, wealthier and stronger, but we experience joy only as sporadic flashes, practically insignificant moments. The 'success', instead of helping us to find happiness, prolongs our agony. Slowly but surely, we become shadows of who we truly are. We lose the meaning of life, the harmony and the inner peace. We feel vulnerable, lacking connection and meaning in the universe.

How did we arrive at this point of total distraction, entangled by so many desires and forgetting what is most important? This compulsive dissatisfaction within us brings a cloud of dark neurosis upon ourselves. To get out of that state of mind which feels like a prison, we need to start with an honest admission of our own participation, our own guilt. That admission will bring clarity and will start the process of liberation from the prisons we have built so painstakingly for ourselves.

Your personal search for meaning, joy and abundance starts with an inner journey. That's just the way it is. And if I tell you now that the starting point is the same as the arrival, you may be disappointed. So let's put that aside for a moment. The secret is in the journey, and it comes with a hidden promise: the ability to see every single facet of life in a new, miraculous way.

This is a journey where you will be asked to knock at doors leading to the darker rooms of your inner being. It will also raise your hopes and then, the very next moment, you might feel that all your dreams have turned to dust. Why? Why not? Is it not among ruins that we find most treasures, as Rumi, the poet, proclaimed? It is in the darkness of the deep soil that the seed of a new future germinates. A brighter future has its roots in today's suffering.

When starting on this journey, it is important to have help from a teacher, a master or someone else who has already experienced something similar, who has already conquered those demons, who has fought those battles and succeeded. By doing this, you will find it easier to motivate yourself and to learn from your past mistakes.

Sometimes, in moments of trial, the only possibility to find light is to go deeper into the darkness. If you've ever lost your way inside a dark place, you know that you have no other option than to go all the way, looking for a shimmer of light. Likewise, going inside your cave and looking for that spark has the potential of bringing hope and creating a brighter future. A new dimension of *you*. It involves a process of surrender, of becoming empty so that you can then fill your own self with a new joy of living. Living in the *now*, one day at a time.

When you let go of your desires and your concerns about what you lack, you see the gift you've been given: the gift of today. The gift of *now*. Have you heard the story of the young, impatient disciple of the old wise man? One day, the disciple came to the banks of a deep river. He wondered for hours what to do and how to cross this great obstacle. He was ready to give up when he saw the wise man on the other side of the river. The young man shouted over, 'Teacher, can you tell me how to get to the other side?' The wise man thought for a moment, then shouted back, over the roaring waters: 'My son, you *are* on the other side.' Like the young man in the story, many times we are already on the 'right side,' on the 'other side'.

Impatience is rooted in the frustration of not finding the answer when a solution is needed. Our impatience is a defence mechanism, a way of deflecting the fear of not finding the answer, the fear of not fitting in. For this reason, impatient people are too discouraged to go inside very deeply. Finding the correct answers requires a leap of faith and consciousness. If only you could wait, then open your eyes and see clearly. Patience is what makes the difference.

Another benefit of a clear mind is admitting your own contribution to what makes you suffer. Many times, we create the suffering, and, even more, we continue to feed it with negative thoughts. To let go of blaming and of judging is liberating. When our understanding deepens, it increases the love we give and receive. Love and understanding go hand in hand.

It helps seeing life with new eyes. Regardless of your state of mind, your heart is patiently waiting to heal, to receive light and to shine its radiance onto others. This is sharing. When you keep everything for yourself, something will always be missing. When you give yourself to others and share everything, in the end, even with empty hands, you still have plenty left in the heart.

The fear of losing seems to bother many people. Here is the good news: when you live in the present moment, you know that what's truly yours cannot be taken away from you. There are more important things in life than what is material, tangible. When you are at peace with yourself and those around you, everything else you need will come. You will see opportunities and will know when to step in or step out. In that very moment, you begin to relax and enjoy life to its fullness.

It is not how much you possess that will make you smile but rather how much you enjoy the smallest thing you have. Experiencing that moment of joy, you realise that what you feel in your heart cannot be stolen or taken away. That moment of bliss will free you, and you will enjoy life and your relationships even more because you will understand that nothing is permanent. It is exactly that absence of fear that will help create and attract your dreams, the vision, the friends and the partner in your life.

Here lies the key to your transformation. Achieving a clear mind comes with the realisation that the present moment is the most important. Living in the present brings a peace of mind that is truly transforming. Fear vanishes, and acceptance and peace fill in all the negative space. The secret is this: the moment you achieve something, detach yourself immediately. Yes, it was your effort, and your accomplishment. Feel grateful. Enjoy it, but at the same time, let it go. When you want to hold onto the old as you embrace the new, it's like trying to sit on two chairs at once. Believe me, you will eventually get stuck or fall through. Make up your mind. Then, believe in yourself.

We must believe in our future despite not being able to see it clearly or in exactly the way we want it to happen. I don't think that we're meant to understand life all the time, but we can all achieve a new level of understanding and self-knowledge. And I think that sometimes we just have to have faith, to believe that after a storm the rainbow will appear.

I speak from my own experience, from the most painful crisis of my life. In autumn 2016, on the day of my birthday actually, I signed the contract for a school renovation, in North Dublin. I ended up working many months for nothing, just to pay the subcontractors hired to finish the job. The job was out of my league, and, combined with lack of experience, my mental strength started to suffer.

I was free-falling and sliding fast toward an unknown grey area, ready to swallow me like a puff of air. I felt things around me falling apart. Falling apart and crumbling. Because of the situation, my marriage was under severe stress. At home, I was like a raging bull, ready to fight the very people I loved most, just because they asked me about my day. My life's foundation was crumbling fast, in front of my very eyes. I felt low, that I had let the family down. I felt broken. I was not only financially bankrupt, but, what was worse, I was emotionally and spiritually empty. I could not see myself falling down any further. That was when I hit the bottom. It was real. It was hard. This was it, the end of the road, and it felt in my heart like a TOTAL ECLIPSE.

One Saturday, in January 2017, while approaching the final stages of the school renovation, I was driving on the M50 motorway, listening to Newstalk radio station. The host, Bobby Kerr, said, 'After the break, I will have in the studio a person who lost 200 million and now is back in business. His name is Keith Cunningham.' When the guest came on, I was struck by the similarity between him and myself. Everything he said resonated with me, within me. At the end of the conversation, Keith said that he would be in Dublin at the Pendulum Summit conference the following Wednesday and Thursday. Never having been to a conference of that kind, I bought the ticket without thinking too much about it.

It was at that event that I met motivational speaker and coach Jack Canfield. I guess the teacher feels the readiness of the student and is attracted by their cry for help and transformation. In June 2017, I went to Jack's retreat in Tuscany. I started to do motivational speaking, and in 2018, I became a member of the Professional Speaking Association Ireland. This led me to the hypnotherapy course run by the Institute of Clinical Hypnotherapy and Psychotherapy Ireland. And this course opened new horizons in my life.

I am grateful to *all* those teachers and masters who helped me to bounce back and synchronise the mind, soul and body with the whispers of the universe.

That building contract may have gone horribly wrong for me, but the crisis delivered to me, as if on a platter, a completely new outlook on life. Three years after those traumatic and life-changing events,

I opened a hypnotherapy clinic in Finglas, Dublin 11. Three years after that, I'm putting the finishing touches on the second clinic, in Castleknock, Dublin 15.

Only by looking back do I realise that there was a connection between the events that unfolded and that specific day: my birthday. Coincidence, you say? It wasn't a coincidence. There are no coincidences. I would rather call it synchronicity. I would not be where I am today without having had that experience. By connecting the dots, retrospectively, I realised the continuity in my chain of existence. Those impactful events were nothing other than opportunities for the rebirth of the soul. How easy it is to miss the obvious when we are half asleep. They were wake-up calls for a transformation.

The crisis made me realise that many of my perceptions – about life, time, success, failure – were quite simply incorrect. For the first time in my life, I could see and feel the past right in front of me. It was as if the heavy curtains that separate the past, present and future suddenly evaporated. There was a moment of shock but also of wonder and awe. I saw life from a completely different perspective.

Then it just hit me. What if I decided to give up controlling everything in my life and to surrender to this new vision? So, I did just that. The consequences of that surrender have been enormous. Things started to happen for me from that moment on. Once we experience flashes of a new reality, we see what's truly possible, and we begin a journey without return. It was at that moment, when I hit the bottom and could not sink any deeper, that I decided to use all my energies and abilities to help others, without thinking of myself at all.

What's it like to have this kind of experience? To be perfectly honest, it is terrifying. First, you become detached from your past. It's like you are no longer able to understand your old self. Only through the encouragement of those who had similar experiences and who understood what I was going through did I find the strength to continue. Second, the sense of isolation and loneliness was very real – almost palpable. I couldn't ignore it, so I felt like I had no choice but to go all the way to understanding what was hiding behind the agony. And I'm glad that I did, even though it required a lot of patience and many sleepless nights.

You can see life in one of two ways: either nothing is a miracle or everything is a miracle. I have seen miracles happening in the lives of my clients, people changing in ways that nobody thought possible. They all had one thing in common, and it had nothing to do with their age or status in life. They all came to me at a breaking point in their lives. Overpowered. Overwhelmed. Their lives seemed to have stopped in their tracks. One of them described it like being in a dream, wanting to run but feeling paralysed. It felt like being crushed by life itself, heavy like living at the bottom of the ocean. So how do you see life right now? The good news is that once you hit the bottom, the only way is up.

For me, there is no doubt in my mind: to be successful is to know yourself. Socrates, Plato and other spiritual leaders and prophets all preached the same thing: Know yourself. The kingdom of Heaven is in your heart. The mystics taught us that looking at the world through a lens of love and understanding can create a brighter, better future. How to get there from where you are today is the purpose of this book.

I have discovered that the process of attracting anything good in your life is governed by eight universal laws: the laws of manifestation. To manifest your intentions, your desires and dreams, you must master all of the laws, although not all with the same intensity.

The daily practice of these laws will remove the unconscious obstacles, will raise awareness and change perception. It will help you create a new reality by showing you how to get your priorities right. And then the biggest mystery of your life will start to be revealed: the miracle of yourself.

Look at the humble lump of coal, black and uneven, the result of millennia of patient fossilisation. It looks like a shiny stone, but in a stove it produces fire, warmth and light. In the right environment, it can even put a turbine in motion, producing electricity. Yes, the coal is incredibly powerful in its own way, full of energy. It's OK to be coal.

Coal and diamonds have an identical chemical composition, but their internal structures are completely different. Diamond molecules are neatly organised – this is why they are so hard and look crystal-clear. Coal molecules are randomly stacked, giving coal its colour and the property that it burns. It can also be easily broken into smaller pieces. Yes, coal is useful, but it is ordinary and breakable. Diamond is extraordinary, solid, hard, rare and precious because it has stood the test of time.

Which would you prefer to be? A piece of coal? Or a diamond?

The shape of the diamond came to me through multiple visions I had during my morning meditations. I started journaling the shapes I was seeing during my visualisations. Finally, I had the curiosity to google them and was surprised to see that many of the shapes in my journal were from Hermetic times, from Ancient

Egypt, and were known as 'Sacred Geometry'. Once, while in a meditative state, reflecting on my journey from the dark night of the soul, the shape of an eight-faced diamond came to me. Around it was a field of energy, spiralling flakes of floating energy in the shape of DNA, spinning anticlockwise, with colours more intense than seven rainbows. A symphony of sound started with the soothing chirping of a cricket, followed by echoes of bells and a flute. The crystal-clear diamond was in the middle, as if the whole universe was radiating from a single point of light: the south point of the diamond, giving birth to everything.

At that moment, the boundaries of my being completely disappeared. I could not perceive myself, Ben, as *Ben*, but as a feeling of TOTAL ONENESS. I was everything. I was that light and the grain of sand melting into the light. My heart filled with an intoxicating silent joy that brought me to tears. The higher I rose and floated, lighter and lighter, the more my tears were overflowing. I knew this feeling was a sign from the universe, showing me the synchronisation and the alignment between the mind-soul and the great truth of nature. I had felt it so many times before.

In a state of inner stillness, I filled each side of the sacred geometrical figure of the diamond with what I thought were the most important universal laws, the ones that helped and guided me to find the true meaning of a purposeful life.

To transform yourself into a beautiful diamond, you need to surrender, to organise your life and to let light shine through your sufferings and limitations. Sometimes it is suffering that provides the pressure that transforms the ordinary, like the coal, into the extraordinary, like the diamond. Our strength comes from accepting the pain and suffering as integral to what we are, part of the dance of life, without discriminating between joy and darkness, without discarding the unknown as something to fear.

When you embrace this change, you can achieve something extraordinary, like transforming coal into a diamond. When you have the courage to connect the dots of your own path in life, you are in for a big surprise. It's akin to discovering a source of perpetual energy: inner peace. With that peace comes the courage to take the next step and the clarity to create something new.

So, today, march as far as you can go. Tomorrow, start again. Every day you will start afresh. Again and again. Whatever one person can do, you can do, too. Just keep the intention in your heart pure and you can achieve anything you want. When things become difficult, do not try to find excuses. Remember, you still have untapped potential and abilities. Dig a bit deeper, and you'll find the living water you are looking for. Now quench your thirst and go further.

The problem with our generation is not digging deeper. We want to enjoy the prize before winning the match. We want to enjoy the results first and only then put in the hard work. This is a recipe for disaster. Our old habits need to change to suit the new circumstances. To achieve anything of importance, you have to change, as it were, the very substance of your thoughts, their very essence. This is not an easy process. It is like being in the middle of a storm, inviting a butterfly to land in the open palm of your hand. If you still remember your childhood when you chased butterflies, you should know that catching a butterfly is not that easy even on a calm, sunny day. Imagine trying it in the middle of a storm. So, for now, just sit still and try to stop the noise in your mind. This is the best way to attract that elusive butterfly, or that dream, or success. You call it anything you want because the name does not matter. Deciding what you want to do next is what matters.

Use this book as a compass to point you towards your own North Star. This journey will lead you to a better understanding of yourself. More clarity means a new level of consciousness, a new understanding that will bring a deeper love for yourself and for those around you. The life you always wanted, the life you were destined to live is waiting for you.

Chapter 1

The law of service

I slept and dreamed that life was joy.
I awoke and saw that life was service.
I acted and behold, service was joy.

—Rabindranath Tagore

I do my share of the housework, but when my wife, Vasi, and our daughter, Julia, do the cleaning, the house truly sparkles. To show my appreciation for their work, every time I enter the house, inside the porch, I take off my shoes.

One time, when I was in the building business, I got a call from a client in Dalkey, in south Co. Dublin, a place where the mountains meet the sea in an unforgettable Celtic landscape embrace. After I showed up at the door, I was invited in. In front of me was a stunning solid-glass staircase, a marvel of architecture, a beautiful piece of art. I knelt down, close to the entrance, and started to untie the laces of my safety boots.

Patiently, the owner, Fran, watched me leave my boots at the door. She noticed my socks, and we both started to smile when we realised that I was wearing odd socks. 'It's your lucky day,' Fran said, and we walked through the house, with her showing me the jobs requiring my attention and me making mental calculations of materials and labour.

Afterwards, Fran, her husband, Jimmy, and I had a cup of coffee in the living room. I was mesmerised by the magnificent view, looking out at the sea. It did not take long to agree on a price and a starting date, and we sealed the deal the old-fashioned way with a firm handshake. That handshake marked a long business relationship between us that lasted more than twelve years.

One day, I asked Fran what made her accept my services so quickly. 'You were the only builder who left his boots at the door before entering the house,' she said. I guess treating other people's property with the same respect as you would your own pays off.

I started implementing this principle in my businesses and when dealing with my customers, and my clients noticed. I was doing more than they expected from me, at no extra cost. For whatever extra they received from me, I only accepted one type of payment: kindness. And kindness attracts kindness.

One day, a very good client of mine, Dermot F., now also a loyal friend, asked me, 'Ben, do you own your own house?' I was renting at the time, and he inquired how much money I had in savings. The next day, he introduced me to a bank manager, and in three short months my wife and I moved into our first home.

In 2008, we added to the landscaping and building business by opening a crèche. Later, in 2013, we expanded, adding two more classes. I enjoyed my work, and I liked not being concerned about the financial aspect of the business. In a world that measured humans' worth only by their financial success, I put people first instead of money. I was present and focused. And the more I immersed myself in and concentrated on serving my customers, the more detached I became. The work and the money kept on coming and coming.

I was not aware of this aspect of my business until an estate agent, John C. from Clontarf, drew it to my attention. I had been working with John for the best part of ten years. Whenever he was selling a house, I took care of the landscaping: clearing the garden and making sure it looked great, both in the sales pictures and in reality. One day, John stopped by and asked me, 'Ben, how come you are doing these jobs for me and you can afford not being paid on time? I have to remind you to send me the invoice for your last job. It looks like you have forgotten altogether about the money.'

The answer to his question was, 'Trust,' one of the most important aspects of human interaction. I trusted John as a partner. He repaid me with the same currency.

I do not work for free, and I am not saying that you should not charge your customers a fair price for your work. Remember, your service is vital for your community, and if you go bankrupt or don't have a job tomorrow, that is not a great result. So, there is a line not to cross there, a fine balance to be achieved. Be wise. But when you put people first, success will follow. It's only a matter of time.

Every time I arrive at a customer's house for a business meeting, even before I ring the bell, I use a simple visualisation exercise: I 'shower' them with appreciation, and then, during our meeting, I focus on them 100 per cent. Being deeply involved in our conversation and focusing only on the person in front of me, it is easy to forget the purpose of the meeting. That is what happens when you are more interested in the person than in their wallet.

Focusing on the person does not mean that the purpose of the meeting becomes obsolete. It means that I am not concerned only with the financial aspect. That takes a lot of tension and anxiety away from the outcome. Closing the deal becomes secondary to the sharing of blessings and the bounty of life. If you apply this simple principle, the deals will come, and customers will want to do business with you, again and again.

The tragedy of humankind today is falling in the trap of the materialistic world, considering it the only reality. Trying to make sense of this life just through the perception of our five senses will take us off course, and our journey through life can become a rough trip. But by focusing on serving others to the best of our ability, we enter a dimension beyond the perception of our physicality, beyond our mundane five senses.

Many people go through life thinking: *my* house, *my* car, *my* wage or *my* job. But these are only temporary things and transient roles our society is imposing on us. When you are operating on the individual ego level and not on the universal level, you think that you can do everything by yourself, on your own. We get too attached to the material world, building walls around ourselves and our possessions. To think this way is to be completely confused.

The truth is that we are more than our possessions and our professional achievements. When we realise that everything belongs to God, including our lives, we will have a smooth ride through life. If, on the other hand, we don't understand that everything belongs to God and not to us, life will be a source of suffering instead of joy. We must have a sense of detachment. If you stay attached to everything material and at the same time try to be free, you will become despondent. You are created to be free. A free human being knows that our potential is limitless. The moment we attach an outcome to our actions, the bliss disappears like dust through our fingers.

There was a point in my life when I thought that everything I produced, earned or created was mine and mine alone to keep. To think like that is like putting the cart in front of the horse. Don't expect it to work. It won't. Later, life showed me that the more I shared my skills and knowledge, the more my heart was filled with joy.

In 1991, I was working in Germany, in Überlingen near Lake Constance, as a chef in a famous Italian pizzeria. The father of the two brothers who owned the restaurant asked me one day how come I was enjoying the work so much. I was so immersed in my job, I hadn't realised that I had been working without a day off for over four months. I was able to keep on going, day after day, week after week.

One thing is certain: living in the present moment, and being aware of it, brings a freshness to your life.

You become more productive; the solutions to problems flow effortlessly towards you. You start smiling and singing. People around you want to eat the same food as you eat or to drink the same holy water, to do whatever you're doing so they can also get a 'taste' of that tremendous energy.

God gave each of us a set of skills and gifts to ease our journey and to fulfil our life contract. Every one of us has a specific talent, but this is a gift to be discovered and then shared, not something to be hidden, buried or kept for ourselves. Do what you came here to do. When you put all your effort into serving your fellow men and women, you are in service of something higher than yourself. This is the best way to fulfil your part of the bargain, your destiny and contract. Now the separation is over, and your activities are meaningful and fulfilling. You become an instrument in the hand of God, and whatever you do has a transformational quality, to you and to your brothers and sisters.

When you are deeply immersed in something you love doing, there's no such thing as time, and all you have is the present moment, the *now*. You are not concerned about future challenges that might come your way. You are brushing aside all worries – everything that blocks your path and is not in alignment with your plan. Whatever humble position you find yourself in, even if you are a part-time kitchen porter, your service is a vital piece in the larger puzzle of creation. By doing whatever you are doing with passion, you are contributing to the greater good that surrounds us. This way, the desire of any human being for a deeper union with God or the universe is being satisfied.

There is great meaning to be found in this kind of attitude. Before you know it, what you do daily – many people call it work – becomes not just a service but an honour, a duty and a mission. When you start every single morning with this attitude, you make God your business partner. In that moment, your life is being transformed. What follows after that people call 'success', but deep in your heart you know it is just a conversation with a higher dimension. Simply put, it is through serving and helping others that you fulfil your destiny. Even in the most mundane job, when you focus more on serving than on just selling, you create the foundation for your future. When we don't share these gifts, we bring harm to ourselves. When we get too attached to material stuff, the ego takes over, and the only outcome is unhappiness, worry and anxiety.

One of my daily business tasks is to connect everything I will do that day with a higher power, a greater good – call it God, Buddha or Allah, what matters to me is that in my mind the work for that day is offered and has a greater purpose. This works very well for me. Before I eat, before I start a job or before any other activity during the day, I offer it first to God. Starting the day with this very simple attitude does not change the course of my plan or activity. The day flows smoothly, effortlessly. When every little thing becomes an offering, I become a detached witness, an instrument in the hands of God. Being an instrument of creation makes us understand that we own nothing. Even our life is God's gift, and we are enjoying everything with his permission.

To do the offering, you have to be anchored in the present moment and not be obsessed with the end result. That way, no matter what you do next will be a win-win situation. This detachment from the outcome gives you a lot of peace of mind and deepens your trust, faith and devotion in the universe, in God.

It doesn't mean you do not care or that you are not focused on improving the service you provide. Yes, you do care, but you trust that the plans will go well. The more you offer the activity to serve others, the more detached you become. Your job, the service you provide, becomes an enjoyable exchange of energy. It requires a new set of habits and changes at every level. For example, you might be sleeping less, if that is what it takes to reach that mark. But the joy, the laughter and the pure intentions from your heart will become part and parcel of what you do, day in, day out. This attitude will change everything.

Being of service is the foundation of true success. So, everything that is good in your heart, don't keep for yourself. Share it, give it away and do not expect anything in return. Believe me, once you drop all expectations, something magic happens.

Being of service to your brother or sister or neighbour is the only thing that will give you purpose, focus and meaning in life. Each day becomes a new page in the book of life, a new point of departure. When you genuinely focus on helping people's problems with your unique set of skills and do your best to forget about the financial aspect, miraculously, the by-product of that attitude is abundance and riches beyond your imagination. I know it might be difficult to believe. You will not believe it until you try it and experience it for yourself.

In the end, the real measure of success is to be the best possible version of yourself. You will become a magnet for goodness, kindness, meaning and purpose. Maybe you've already met someone like this. Some people are like living magnets, attracting and giving away kindness, goodness and empathy. Being in their presence is quite an experience. There is nothing stopping you from becoming such a person.

The good news is that you already *are* that person, only you may not know how to bring this side of you to the surface. Yet.

Being ready to serve others requires vulnerability and courage: the courage to know who you really are. It's not always easy to show your true self. But by doing just that, communicating with your fellow humans gets easier and better. Your vulnerability works like an icebreaker for the person in front of you. When feelings change, their thinking changes too. And it's not only them changing. You change as well. When you uproot all doubts and fears from within, everything changes. This is the real miracle, one that will not only send shockwaves to your system, but the magnitude of that transformation will be seen by those around you, too.

Joy is everything. Feeling the 'hand of God' and participating in the creation of this world, you realise that God is the breath inside your breath, the scent behind the rose you are seeing, the whisper you are hearing inside your heart and the life beyond your life. For this reason, focus not on what others are doing but only on what you can do. By looking inside, you start a chain reaction. Look with clarity to what you already have in terms of skills and blessings, then multiply it by eleven. If you have to start a new course, to acquire a new skill, just go ahead. Do it and keep the big picture in mind. As soon as you start, you will understand that today there are more choices than you imagined yesterday. Tomorrow there will be other new opportunities. This is what this transformation will do to you.

If I am responsible for the world I see, that means I am the 'creator' of that world. This is an incredible calling and a great privilege. By putting all your skills and talent to work to help others, you put your heart and passion in the service of God. The result is that worries, doubts and fears magically evaporate. This is not a small feat. It is a supreme act of devotion that will run through your entire being, through what you think, say and do during each day of service. So, your priority is to bring joy and smiles to those you are serving.

Focus all your energy into bringing joy to others. The first visible result is that of letting go of what you think is your just reward. Let go. Trust. Create. Be who you are. On this journey, you don't need to be in control of everything. Occasionally, you might need to take your hands off the 'steering wheel of life'. There are other forces at work too. They will help you succeed. Serve your community to the best of your ability. This will bring you closer and closer to your true self. Once you commit your heart and soul to that task, help appears in your life from nowhere. You trigger a process of remembering pieces of the great puzzle that was your life before, and now you get the whole image. Suddenly, it makes sense. Life is now exciting and more fun. You become more patient with yourself and with those around you. You are not hurt easily any longer. You are at peace.

The final piece of knowing yourself and reaching your full potential is putting all your energy to help others, to heal divisions and to bring a smile. This will grant you access to a higher form of wisdom, love and understanding. The task requires total commitment and faith, but, believe me, whatever life throws at you, you will be okay. You will be fine. You will do well no matter how the future unfolds. Your heart will embrace your ego with love, and this will result in an emptied ego and your life being devoted to a greater good.

The best antidote for an inflated ego is to focus on giving. Start by asking a simple question: 'What can I do for others today?' The answer might require a new start, like upgrading your skills, finishing what you are doing now and starting a totally new job. If you feel the call in your heart, go for it. You know that this new path will give you joy and new purpose in life. You just have to love to serve more than you love the reward. Because it's not about the immediate profit. This type of service, helping others, will give you a sense of humility and will make you see the world with new eyes, every single day, as if seeing it for the first time. This is a small miracle that you will witness every morning. Every day always new, every day always fresh, without the bloated residue of yesterday's memory.

With this new set of skills, you are participating in the building of a new type of society and relationships. You will see for yourself: you will experience joy in life like never before. Creating, connecting and serving others bring great spiritual rewards and become the essence of real growth. Money, a full wallet, as a type of reward, is not part of the bargain any longer. But you will not lack anything. This attitude will bring bliss and meaning to your existence. You can consider your offering as a surrender to God, and once you reach this stage, you will not be concerned anymore about amassing a fortune because you will attract financial rewards anyway. This kind of attitude (and a bit of wisdom) means that success follows everywhere you go.

The reward for following this call is great. It is not what you get for it but what you become. Life, when lived this way, will give you much more than you are expecting from it. The whole process is magnetic and prophetic. When we start the day with this reverence for life and for your brother and sister, our treasures do not diminish. In fact, more is given to you in the form of new ideas, abundance and joy. Doors will open, more business will come your way in your professional life, and you will gain more than you expect.

There are so many men and women who have been discarded by others. Find and help them: those who think little of themselves, who have buried the gift they received at the moment of birth. Serve those most in need. Guide and help those who have lost the path. Make them believe in themselves again. Show them that their inner light is still burning bright. Give them a new direction. Most of all, give them *hope*. That person will come back to life. When you give hope, you perform a real miracle.

In helping others to hope and to believe in themselves again, you will find your own joy. Your heart will be filled to the brink, and that is more precious than any bank account or any piece of property that you might acquire. When you heal the hearts of others, your soul heals too. It transforms, it grows, it changes. It is this radiant light that creates more positive energy. When you support, strengthen and encourage others, you also receive guidance, inspiration and beauty for yourself. By doing this, you are fulfilling your mission and performing a small miracle. In that moment, you become an instrument of God.

Remember

- Show your appreciation for other people's service.
- When you put other people first, success will follow.
- Being of service is the foundation of true success.
- It is through serving and helping others that you fulfil your destiny.
- The real measure of success is to be the best possible version of yourself.

Chapter 2

The law of forgiveness

The wound is the place where the light enters you.

—Rumi

They say that you will always smile remembering your first love, and I suppose this is true, but is there such a thing as a sad smile of remembrance? Of course there is. I fell in love for the first time during the summer of 1985, just before starting my military service. A beautiful girl called Graziela stole my heart and made me dream with my eyes wide open. That summer went by in a blink of an eye. Immediately after my service, I started my first year at the university in Iași, about eighty kilometres from my home village.

I was happy with us having a long-distance relationship, and we kept the flame of love burning by means of letters and visits. But the years went by, and we found it more and more of a struggle to carry on our relationship. Trying to be together while living apart was tough.

I was the one who first drifted away. I started to see someone else, and I eventually stopped writing and visiting. When I saw Graziela again, I realised the impact and the magnitude of the hurt I had inflicted on her. I had ruined a relationship which she saw as sacred and unique. I was not proud of myself. I went home that night, and I wrote a short letter in which I begged her forgiveness. The next day, I went to her house. I said hello, put the letter on the table in front of her and left.

In 2019, after twenty-eight years waiting for an answer, I wrote and sent Graziela another letter. I made sure she would get it. I found out that she was married, with children, and that she was living in Italy. I also found out that she was suffering from cancer. I rang her, and she accepted to take a call from me. It wasn't an easy conversation. Even after all that time, there was still hurt, guilt and regret.

Over the course of our conversation, I found out that she had never seen the letter I had written her all those years ago. Was it taken away by one of her parents? Who knows?! But she never saw or read it, and she was as surprised as me when I mentioned it to her. We had the strength to make peace, to forgive each other and to embrace the future. Graziela survived her illness and is now on the road to recovery. And I learnt the grace of forgiveness, twenty-eight years after hurting someone.

The law of forgiveness is very simple: you cannot receive what you refuse to give. Our inner selves, to realise their full potential, first have to be forged in the flames of forgiveness. There is no other way. Only forgiveness and understanding will transform fear, anger and jealousy into a love that radiates kindness, allowing us to smile again.

Instead of seeking an outside cure for our emotional turmoil by pointing the finger at the person who hurt us yesterday, or patching the hurt with more time spent suffering, it is better to make contact with our real self and to experience forgiveness fully. This might involve reaching out and giving the gift of forgiveness to the other person. It is a gift you give to yourself too. What you discover in the process might pleasantly surprise you. In forgiving, we get to know who we really are, and we can communicate it to those around us.

The biggest obstacle in the process of finding peace and ending the turmoil of the heart is self-forgiveness. Looking for forgiveness before you forgive yourself will only prolong your suffering. So, self-forgiveness first. This will lead you to forgive others and to receive forgiveness from them. Remember, too, that if you can't forgive yourself, you will never be able to forgive other people.

If you think you are not worthy of this precious gift, you are judging yourself too harshly. This is a reflection of what you think of other people, and it is a trick of the mind. By judging someone else, you feel that others judge you with the same measure. But an eye for an eye will create a community of blind people, unable to enjoy the colours and miracles of life.

Our inability to forgive ourselves is a great obstacle. We cannot feel the gift of transformation until we clear the heavy burdens obstructing our own path to forgiveness.

The belief that we are unforgiven and unforgivable is a tremendous source of suffering. Every person has a purpose in this life, and so do you. You are worthy of being loved and forgiven. The best thing is to forgive in your heart even before the person asks for your forgiveness. Someone who has hurt you might not know of the pain they have inflicted on you. Forgive anyway. And when forgiveness is asked explicitly, give it with all your heart. If that person had grown in a better environment, they would have acquired a different way of looking at life. They would have behaved differently altogether. Make it as clear as possible that everyone has to move on. That that place will never be revisited.

Forgiving someone gives you tremendous power over the other person. You are free while they might still be in chains. This shouldn't make you arrogant. The moment you set that person free, your own heart will be charged with positivity. Whatever shadow, pain and hurt you carried within will be transformed into light.

The alchemists in the old legends and stories were known for their ability to transform lead into precious gold. The moment you forgive the person who hurt you and made you suffer, you become an alchemist. And the more you forgive, the more you increase the light and love in your life. You transform pain and suffering into a radiating love coming from your soul. All shadow, torment and hurt are now changed into a precious feeling of being at peace. How do you know that you are ready to liberate the person who hurt you? The best clue is that your feelings towards the person who hurt you change. You feel no grudge and no resentment, no matter how deep the scars.

There is no guarantee that the person you hurt in the past is ready to drop the heavy burden of holding on to that resentment. You give yourself the best chance to move on once you pass through the 'gate' of self-forgiveness. By doing that, you open a window towards the person suffering. This is why it is impossible to be forgiven unless we forgive first. It might take time until the other is ready, but at least you started a chain reaction in the subconscious mind of the person living in agony.

Forgiveness always comes from the heart. The mind will try to reason about it and maybe put forgiveness aside, but the heart will embrace forgiveness. There is a golden thread going through every human heart, connecting us. We are as one, and the moment you communicate better with yourself, forgiveness asserts its presence and we are ready to ask it from the person we hurt.

Seeking forgiveness is not always easy or straightforward, and it takes courage, but remember: what you seek, you already are. If you really want to be forgiven, do not let the mind distract the heart's plan by overthinking everything. Listen to your heart.

Asking for forgiveness will open all kinds of invisible doors for you. The moment the heart embraces the mind, and the two work together, we discover a new dimension of ourselves. The more we understand the effects of our choices, the more we tap into our infinite resources to love. The more we love, the more we understand. And the deeper the level of understanding, the more profound is our love.

Every experience of your life is necessary to balance the energies of your mind, body and soul. So stop pointing the finger at whoever or whatever happened yesterday. You cannot stay forever in your cave blaming your parents, your education or the government for your habits. I know this because I made the same mistakes. While I was living on the east side of the Berlin Wall, I pointed the finger at the Communist regime. I blamed others. I did not want to take any responsibility for my failures. I realised that in order to find a way forward, I had to forgive and forget the old self.

You, too, have to learn to live in the present, especially when the past is painful. Forgive and move on; wake up, the sleep is over. Being present in the now opens the door to your new life. Step out of your old life and embrace the new and the now. Likewise, the time to practise forgiveness is now. Today. If you find yourself getting caught up in the tricks of the mind endlessly dragging you into the past, reclaim your powers by anchoring yourself back in the present moment.

Refuse to feed the remorse or pain of the past. You can meditate or pray or be still; become aware of the present moment until inner peace is achieved. Sometimes, all you need is just a few brief moments: this will be enough to feed the soul for the whole day.

If someone hurt you in the past, it does not mean that you can't change the meaning of that event. You need to see everything into a new light: the light of love and generosity. If you can't let go, you allow the past to be in the driver's seat of the future. The beautiful diamond that is your soul will remain stained and dull until you are ready to free others and move on.

Choosing to remain stuck in the past is like carrying heavy bags of sand for two people. The burden will eventually exhaust you. Not letting the burden go will distort and contaminate all your actions with bitterness. But letting go means that you will stop bringing the emotional weight of the past event into today.

Feeling bitter will have a negative impact on your ability to have healthy relationships with people. Have you ever wondered why some people prefer living in a painful past instead of letting go? We are all coming from the same source, but along the way we pick up habits and beliefs that can be hurtful to others. These habits work like a pair of spectacles that distort what we see and how we understand the world. Letting go of the past is like taking off those glasses and throwing them away. When you reach this point in your life, you understand that pain, heartache and suffering are all windows open towards awareness. When we reach this point of understanding, we stop reacting to negative feelings and start creating moments and relationships of love and reverence.

Instead of closing your heart and locking it in a prison, these experiences, painful as they might be, can awaken your spirit. And being awake spiritually is a gift that helps you understand and love without discrimination. So stop for a moment and ask one simple question: 'How can I change this suffering into something positive? How can I start acting from a place of love and empowerment and quit reacting so aggressively every time someone pushes my buttons?'

When you stop blaming others for your shortcomings, your focus changes. You have a new purpose. Each day, your thoughts, words and actions are in alignment with your life's purpose. This gives you clarity and motivation. Do your best every day, and whatever you do, do it with love and acceptance. As you advance with devotion in discovering the hidden dimensions of yourself, you learn how to create a new life. A new you.

Some people call it an inward journey. I see it more as a process of re-creation than a journey. We have to see our lives not as a chain of events interrupted by hurt and suffering but as a chain of possibilities. The good news is that these external events and forceful reactions from your past are also opportunities to start a fresh, brand-new day. When you see a new day with new eyes, without the burden of yesterday, then we give forgiveness a chance to change the most impossible situations.

Start investing into a life of purpose. If the cause of your suffering was a creation of your imagination, so is the solution to end it. In your mind, you created a disproportionate battle that you will never win by always looking for a scapegoat outside of you.

For many of us, loving and forgiving each other seems just a bridge too far – because we always complicate things. Our mission in this life is very simple: love others as you would love yourself. Forgive others as you would forgive yourself. When you embrace the present moment, you are not only closer to today but closer to the reality that exists in you and around you. One of the best ways to reach peace in our hearts is to seek the truth. It takes great courage to seek the truth and then to accept it. A higher level of mindfulness and awareness is also necessary. Once we reach that point, we better understand the dynamic of the heart. And from that place, we are ready to ask for forgiveness from others.

Many times, one hurtful experience will stop you in your tracks, forcing you to look inside. Reacting to pain, you start to see hidden dimensions of yourself. Finally, you understand that you are more than the pain you experience. It's not an easy path, but by advancing with courage and curiosity, you can start to unwrap those negative emotions. Bit by bit, you can change your perceptions of those events from the past.

As you progress and evolve consciously, those fearful emotions start to peel away as, one at a time, you heal them and change them. You realise that the painful events did not come to punish you but to awaken you and allow you to discover a deeper level of love. Each event offers an opportunity, contributing to the balancing and growth of the soul. This does not mean that only pain brings about the discovery of the real you. Love has the same effect.

This is the reality of life: what happened to us yesterday cannot be denied or changed. But how we react to the outcome today is well within our power. We all have that strength in our heart. Doing just that, you start a transformation in yourself and, by proximity, in the world around you. You become what you've been all along: an alchemist, a magician, transforming a piece of coal into a shining, priceless diamond. You finally understand 'that the wound is the place the light enters you,' as Rumi said so beautifully.

We are more than what we think. We are better, kinder and more resourceful than others think us to be. But we can only discover this hidden potential when we stop dividing and separating, when we stop seeing events as black and white, as win or lose. The pain and suffering, the false images we create about people who hurt us or who we hurt, cannot be viewed in isolation and without an understanding of the true nature of the soul.

Imagine human life as a structure made out of light and colours. Your light is your consciousness, and the intensity of the light radiating from your body is in direct proportion to your level of consciousness and the amount of love flowing from you. When you raise your level of consciousness, you increase the frequency and the intensity of your light. The more consciousness and awareness you have, the more light you radiate from the soul.

The realm of the soul operates differently from what we know with the conscious mind. In most cases, when we forgive, the transformations in us are beyond incredible. Forgiveness continually reminds us that the joy of living is in giving completely because we can only truly give what we have in our hearts. When we give from that place, it comes back to us multiplied, not as a possession but as a feeling. This is the place from where miracles begin to manifest: we attract only what we feel in our hearts. When you reach this point in your journey, you finally realise that Heaven is not a place in a distant land but a feeling, a state of mind and body, created by your soul.

You must learn the art of giving to master the art of living. This dynamic change goes hand in hand with your determination to know yourself. Not everyone is ready for this dramatic shift in perception. Not everyone is ready to believe that they can stop the cycle of negativity and doubts. It requires a total commitment, faith and focus of the mind.

Many times, I see in people a distorted way of forgiving. Let me explain. People think they are being forgiving, but in fact they can't let go completely. In a hidden corner of their mind, they secretly wish that the person will always remain in debt to them. This is not real forgiveness because it's not done with pure intentions. That seed of unforgiveness, left there in the dark, will create remorse, manipulation and control. Choosing not to forgive is like a flower trying to bloom in a dark place. It will wither.

The best thing to do is just love people, regardless of their ability to understand you or not. If they don't understand you, forgive them anyway. Pray for them that one day they too will be able to hear and answer that inner call. Just because you received a call and decided to follow it does not mean that everyone will join you in that inner revolution. This does not make you better than others and has nothing to do with your intellectual abilities. In many cases, the intellect can be a hindrance. Being able to understand and surrender to that call has more to do with the purity of intentions radiating from the heart and not the intellect.

Forgiveness has very little chance without communication. I have learnt that the main reason for emotional pain and suffering is repression and lack of communication. Shutting down the lines of communication is the worst thing we can do. Writing yourself a letter of forgiveness is a great way to fully express your thoughts concerning your past mistakes and to get all your negative emotions and anger out of your system. This letter should help you understand how you feel, putting you in a better position to move forward towards self-forgiveness so you can start a new chapter, by creating a physical distance that allows you to move in the direction of peace and reconciliation.

So, write yourself a sincere letter of forgiveness: 'I forgive myself so that I can forgive others.

Everything good or bad that I've done is in the past. There is nothing I can do to change the past. I accept my lesson and move on with the idea that I will be a better person in the future. I release my past so that I can step into my future. I accept that I did the best I could at the time. Now that I know better, I will do better.' Today, you know better, and you will do better. Use your past actions as opportunities for change and growth. Next time around, when you're in a similar situation, practise what you've learnt to make the outcome better. Say it in a loud voice, three times: 'I forgive myself, and I am ready to move on.'

Forgiveness is a choice and a gift at the same time, a jewel you have to give freely and completely. Give it without manipulation and without expecting to get a gold medal in return. Some people find this difficult or even impossible. The reason for that is because we equate the person who needs our forgiveness with their actions. Follow the soul's path, for this is the only road that brings a smile, inner peace and fulfilment in your life. Learn to still your mind. Remain in unity with your true being and keep your intentions pure and clear. The moment you succeed with these tasks, your heart will embrace everything with love. Have more courage and trust the whispers coming from within. The pure intentions radiating from that embrace will bring the understanding that what you wanted the most was always in front of you.

Remember

- You cannot receive what you refuse to give.
- You are worthy of being loved and forgiven.
- Hurting someone is nothing more than hurting ourselves.
- When you know better, you do better.
- 'I forgive myself, and I am ready to move on.'

Chapter 3

The law of faith

Faith is taking the first step even when you don't see the whole staircase.

—Martin Luther King Jr.

To reach your destination you need an unshakeable faith. I moved to Iaşi in autumn 1986. Away from my parents and my home village, the big city could have been a strange and unforgiving place. Luckily, I had a friend living there. We had both grown up in the village of Săbăoani, in eastern Romania, about 100 kilometres from what was then the border with Russia (now Moldova). My friend was slightly older – and definitely wiser. Because of this, we did not call him by his first name. We simply called him 'The Elder' (*Batrinul*). The name stuck. I cherished his support and advice and cannot emphasise enough the importance of good friendships in life.

It was Batrinul who suggested we get involved with the Scouts group in the local Catholic church, where, during my final year in the university, I came across a little mantra that has helped me immensely throughout my life. That year, for a feast day, the

Scouts organised a play in the church. Each one of us in the group had a role to play and a few lines to deliver. I remember clearly when I was handed an envelope with my part inside. It contained a single line: 'The Virgin Mary taught me to believe even when there is nothing left to believe in.'

To believe, even when you think there is nothing left to believe in. I think that is a beautiful definition of unshakeable faith. That mantra has stayed with me ever since and has been a bright light in the darkest moments in my life. I heard it during my quest for freedom, travelling from East to West, when my life almost left my body as I was crossing mountains and rivers in the bitter cold of winter.

Between 1991 and 1992, I was working illegally, at the Italian restaurant in Überlingen. As a Romanian citizen, I was not allowed to work in another country or travel freely. One morning in July 1992, a tall police officer and a detective stormed into my flat, produced a deportation order and gave me twenty minutes to grab my clothes. The plane was still on the runway in Frankfurt airport when I was already planning the journey back. Back in Romania, I was like a caged lion trying hard to control my anger and disappointment, thinking about my hard-earned savings sitting in a German bank.

That September, I decided to go back. I had a plan to travel Romania–Hungary–Austria–Germany. I decided to cross the border between East and West in one of the most impossible spots: Sopron, a town on the Hungarian–Austrian border. The plan was so risky that my friends back home were placing bets on me, counting the days until I was caught and sent back.

It was almost evening when I arrived in Sopron. I didn't even know what direction the Austrian border was in. But, somehow, I had a deep sense of inner peace and serenity. I felt I could handle the situation. As I was walking away from Sopron's train station, the echo of my mantra sounded in my ears: 'The Virgin Mary taught me to believe, even when there is nothing left to believe in.'

That line crossed my mind when I saw a church. I

went inside. The church was empty. I finished praying, and then I saw a priest bringing a fresh white cloth to cover the altar. He saw me and invited me to sit down with him. I explained in broken German that I was from Romania and that I had been deported from Germany a few months back. I needed to go back to get my money from the bank. I asked him to show me the best place to cross the border. I was tired, and all of my money was spent, but I was ready to continue my journey on foot.

While I was talking to the priest, another man walked into the room. He seemed to be the caretaker of the church. The two men discussed something for less than a minute, and then the priest said to me, 'We will help you.' Before I could say anything, he took out his wallet and emptied it into my hands. The caretaker did the same. They gave me all they had: about 150 US dollars. They even emptied the collection box for me. I couldn't move, I felt so touched – shocked really – by the generosity of these two strangers. I collapsed on my knees and started to cry.

After about six hours of walking through the forest and along the train track, it started to rain. By now, I was in Austria, and the plan was to take a train to bring me close to the German border. I was excited but exhausted and hungry too, and I needed to rest until the morning.

I was sitting in the woods, with my back against a willow tree, next to a little stream, all my wet clothes still on me. Everything was quiet and serene, the moss so soft under my feet and the fresh smell of the pinewood forest filling the air. I fell asleep.

Somehow, I felt that I was floating and everything around me looked really beautiful and peaceful. I was now in a different place. I was seeing natural landscapes like I had never seen before: flowers and rivers, birds and butterflies, and my fingers, trying to touch them, were softly passing through without any resistance, like they were pure spirits or energy. Everything was keeping its shape, and everything was one. There was no track of time, and there was no distance. I felt myself rising higher and higher.

The sky above me was now even brighter, and I really started to enjoy the whole experience.

Then I heard a voice that somehow I knew deep down inside me was the voice of my grandfather, who actually died six years before I was born: 'Baron! Go back! What are you doing here?! Go back before it is too late!'

Suddenly I was awake as if a rock had hit my forehead. All I could hear now was a loud rattle. Confused and disoriented, it took me a few minutes to understand what was going on. I had not only fallen asleep but had gone into a near-fatal hypothermic shock. Because I had never experienced anything like it, I did not realise what it was.

The loud sound was in fact my teeth rattling. I was really scared, and I just could not stop it. I tried everything. I tried praying out loud, singing (sort of), more praying, then walking. I even tried to bite a piece of wood to make it stop. Nothing worked. My whole body was stiff like concrete, and I couldn't bend my arms or legs anymore. Thank God, I had spare clothes with me. In those moments, when most people would panic or retreat in defeat, I clearly heard the echoes of my mantra: 'Believe, even when there is nothing to believe in.' It guided me, like a lighthouse in a storm.

That time in Hungary, I was on my knees, but instead of panic and despair, I felt a deep serenity overflowing from my heart. Just remembering the help the priest and the church caretaker gave me brings tears of gratitude to my eyes even now, thirty years later. To the unknown priest and the caretaker of the church, I just want to say, thank you.

The truth is, the moment I decided to leave my country, to free myself from the shackles of the Communist regime's corruption, nothing and nobody could dissuade me from my vision and my dreams. The search for freedom meant more than just moving from one country to another. It was also a spiritual search. I was seeking to transcend that great dichotomy: the separation between feeling free and feeling burdened by my history, a fate that my parents could not shake off or fight.

On my perilous journey, I put all my trust in Our Lady, and I surrendered completely. I took my hands off the steering wheel. My trust pushed all my worries and doubts away, and I knew, I just knew, that every piece of the puzzle would fall into the right place. It was only a matter of time, of being patient and of waiting for the right path to open up in front of me. This attitude of trust, this *faith*, made all the difference and led me to abundance, freedom and inner peace.

There is a saying that we truly enter the church when we are leaving the church building. There is no point in declaring your faith by only showing up each Sunday. Faith has to be practised daily and with firm devotion. Once you commit to this goal, nothing from the outside should affect you, so don't be influenced by other people's judgements and opinions.

Faith has to be shown in our daily relationships and in our interaction with all living beings, which means not kicking the cat because you feel like it or crushing an insect because you can. Life is sacred, and we have to feel a deep reverence for it. We cannot be the ego-mind, always ready to dominate, to win and come out on top every time we interact with other forms of life. This is the type of illusion we have to discard through practising our faith with devotion.

End the inner conflict by refusing to join the club of negativity. Just because your neighbour is behaving like they did yesterday doesn't mean you have to do it, too. Stop contributing to the pessimistic vibes of fear and anxiety. These might be things that you learnt from your parents. You just need to unlearn them. Let go. Why should we be afraid? Life is all about change. Accept vulnerability and accept change. Change makes you alert and teaches you not to be shackled to your achievements. Accepting change and vulnerability will also loosen the grip of your ego on your soul.

So, where do we start? With our possessions maybe? Have you ever watched a bee collecting nectar? The bee never stops. It seems to have a great enthusiasm and a sense of urgency ingrained into its DNA. We too go through life collecting. We collect things, wealth, money. In doing so, we think that we will be safe. Then, when we reach the desired outcome, our next instinct is to get a tight grip on our possessions. We hold on to them very tightly so we don't lose them. We take measures to make sure that our treasure will not diminish. Instead of enjoying the moment and the gift that life gave us with generosity, we start thinking about the possibility of losing it all tomorrow. When everything we say starts with 'I', 'me', 'mine', 'my property', 'my car', 'my house' and so on, we are heading for a disaster.

We do the same thing with our relationships. We treat the other person as a possession. But building a wall around the one you love marks the end of true love. Such a wall is a reflection of our own heart being imprisoned by fear. Be sure, in terms of how you see your possessions, that you are not a hunter looking for a kill but a farmer in charge of a field. There are indeed wonderful crops that will grow if you work that field.

Nothing is really, truly yours. Everything can be taken away from you tomorrow. You just get to enjoy today's harvest and to eventually pass on that field to someone else.

What defines you has nothing to do with what you own. By focusing only on material things, you are wasting your life, no matter how much you are worth financially in the end. So how do we avoid sleep-walking into this egotistical abyss? How do we lose the grip our possessions have on us? First of all, stop saying like a child: 'mine, mine, mine.' Even this small change will create a ripple effect, and it will allow you to celebrate you being you. Clear, clean, without the fear of losing the head, the heart or your valuable possessions.

Fear and doubt exist in our lives because we are not anchored strongly enough in the present moment. We think we are smart, powerful, rich, but all we have is the gift of today. It is given to us through the grace of the universe, God, nature. Constantly worrying about the future and security is inviting unnecessary trouble into your life. We allow our fears and anxieties to take over, and in that very moment we forget the joy and freshness of the present *now*. And living in the past is as dangerous as living in the future. Laozi said it so beautifully: 'If you are depressed, you are living in the past. If you are anxious, you are living in the future. If you are at peace, you are living in the present.'

For a long time, I did not want to learn the lessons life tried to teach me. I did not want to change the course of my life. Wanting my valuable possessions and achievements to last forever, I was hoarding material riches and squeezing them tight – only for me and close family. And because of this attitude, life sent me an awakening crisis. I learnt, the painful way, that everything I produce is not mine to keep.

When, in 2016, life threw me into a very dark cave, I was not only financially bankrupt, but, what was worse, I was emotionally and spiritually empty. I could not see myself falling any further. I hit the bottom. It was real. It was dark. Hard. This was the end of the road. With no mental strength left, I knew instinctively that my only safe harbour was my faith. And there were times when I felt that this faith had abandoned me as well. This is what is known as 'the dark night of the soul'. Sensing that I had nobody to hear my cry for help, I was faced with the reality of an empty body and an empty mind. Total stillness, no more thoughts to think. My little mantra kept me going: 'The Virgin Mary taught me to believe even when there is nothing left to believe in.'

Eventually, the darkness of the cave became too much to handle. The silence was deafening. After a while, in that raw weakness and vulnerability, I felt a palpable humbleness. The masks finally dropped. This was the point where my ego completely disappeared, and I knew that I was starting something new.

I am an ordinary man from the countryside. Your story might not be the same as mine, but there is really no difference between you and me. Your abilities are probably even greater than mine. We are created to survive and thrive no matter what happens to us. We have the power to lift up all the broken pieces and to build again. All you have to do is to believe in a higher power.

Living in the present moment will keep your awareness sharp and is the only way to get rid of fears and doubts. But to live in the present moment, you need to accept your vulnerability. To be alive is to be vulnerable. If we accept this, we can start enjoying this miracle called life. There is no guarantee what tomorrow will bring so you had better live this present moment of joy and treasure it.

Who knows where that joy will bring you next? Will it make you more generous and fill your heart with love and gratitude? There is a good possibility you can go beyond the limitations of your physicality just by being fully present. How limitless is your body? How many dimensions can your inner eye see?

The soul who reaches this degree of knowledge shows a deep reverence for others. Their simple presence dissipates tensions by radiating forgiveness, love and gratitude. The simplicity emanating from their heart is noticeable to all. Without faith, devotion and humility, you just can't partake in this kind of energy.

The moment you leave behind the worldly urge of achieving, hoarding and possessing things, your struggles will diminish. You surrender, and, as a result, you detach yourself from the daily drama of 'me, mine, myself' and are ready to recognise and embrace your life's mission. Instead of floating aimlessly on the sea of life, suddenly there is new purpose and direction in your sailing. You follow a precise call, and it's like someone is whispering in your ear, 'Everything is going to be all right. Everything is going to be a thousand times better than you have ever expected.' In this acceptance and inner peace, there is unity. A deep sense of trust envelops your heart and mind.

Each one of us has a calling in life, a vocation, but this vision is usually shielded from us from an early age. We are taught to believe that the only existing reality is the one we see with our physical eyes. Nothing could be further from the truth. To really see what lies behind the veil of our five senses, to reach the core of what we truly are, we have to discard what we are *not* in the first place. And to reach your dream, your vision and your goals, no matter how impossible they might seem, you have to start with an unshakeable faith. It is through such faith that all our contradictions and desires are finally satisfied. Only by surrendering to a higher power can you end your inner struggle. Your mind's turmoil clears and settles, and your mind becomes your servant and not a tyrant that rules over you.

To have a solid platform in life, you must build an unshakeable foundation so you can overcome criticism, setbacks and suffering. Like an iceberg, 90 per cent of which is under water, most of your wisdom and stability are deep below the surface, hidden from what people around you can see. That wisdom within will allow you to stay whole and composed in adversity. The negativity, doubts and suffering in our life are all caused by the lack of inner stability.

In a time of a crisis, your true character reveals the full colours of your soul. During a trial, a person guided by love, compassion and wisdom becomes even better. Faith comes from within, and no external events can crush it. No firing squad, no corrupt government can shake that foundation. If you are deeply rooted in faith, nobody can take it from you.

One of the best ways to reach this level of stability is through the daily practice of faith and devotion. By regular prayer and meditation, you develop a new habit of remembering to remain anchored into today. When you sow the pure intentions of morning prayers and meditations in the fertile soil of a faithful heart, you will reap in the harvest of actions. Because of the pure and clear intentions, they become holy.

Without devotion, our faith has no roots. Most people show faith when life is going well. It doesn't take much to do that. But faith can be tested when we hit a rough patch. Then we rebel. We fall into the trap of discarding our faith and doubting the existence of a higher power. If this happens, the faith we thought we had is not genuine. To be genuine in times of trouble, faith has to be practised daily and be reflected in all our activities and attitudes. We have to keep the flame of faith burning within our hearts even when we see no harvest.

To allow the Divine Grace to make a home in your heart is a conscious choice only you can make. That permission and acceptance brings you beyond the human ability to understand, to love and to share – beyond service and duty, beyond sadness and tears of joy. To surrender to the gift, to embrace and follow your life's mission, requires not only courage, simplicity and humbleness. It requires a quantum leap of faith.

If you feel that your prayers are not being answered in exactly the way you want, there is a very good reason for that: the universe has something even better for you in store. The Beloved will shower you with abundance, bliss and joy beyond your ability to comprehend. By trusting Providence's timing, you surrender to his will and become receptive to the whisper felt in meditation. By relinquishing the initial plan, the old frames and maps, you are not bothered anymore by details and timing.

There's only one condition: you must keep the devotion, the trust and the innocence in your heart.

You will make progress even if you do not see it. Why can't you see the progress? Because you *are* the progress. Can you see your sight? Can you hear your hearing? Your progress is the sight behind your sight. You fall and get up again. You trip and stumble. Rise again and keep going. You are much closer to the destination than you think.

Once you start on your own journey, you will find a clarity and an inner peace along the way that will guide you like a lighthouse. You become aware of your soul's immortality, and this gives you a tremendous but humbling power. You will also feel a responsibility to use your power for helping other human beings and all forms of life on the planet. A person with strong faith uses all their energy as part of their service and mission.

You see, the people who surrender entirely to this journey have a different operating system; each one of their steps in life is in line with their life's purpose. They are there to serve others and are not concerned with what other people think of them. From the outside, they might look naive because they are generous givers and are not afraid to prostrate themselves in front of other people. But they are deeply rooted in the present and know that everything they give comes from an abundant source.

When we are open-minded and in a state of receptivity, we prepare the ground to receive gifts beyond our imagination. We allow new possibilities; new guidance is coming our way. We create conditions to receive a new vision for life, one that comes from the depth of our own soul, one that is in alignment with our true mission.

Interestingly, this vision can be revealed to you in the form of an image, a scent, a song or a symbol that will be your guiding light. At this moment, most of us get frightened and retreat. Others simply ignore the sign. The fear and doubts in their hearts overpower it. But their withdrawal can only be temporary because no one can escape their true calling. It can be delayed but not postponed indefinitely. What you seek is in fact seeking you.

You can only do so much on your own. If you need help, all you have to do is ask. Asking for help requires a great deal of inspiration and humility. It is this humbleness and your genuine request that will allow Providence to answer your prayers. When you are suffering but have the courage to say, 'Enough is enough', the best way forward is to look for a teacher or master to help you out. Sometimes, whoever is in front of you is your teacher. A humble earthworm or a leaf falling from a tree: there is a lesson there for you. Only you know what that lesson is.

You are here to enjoy the voyage of discovering your own unlimited potential. With a simple shift in your focus, you can escape from the shackles of fears and enjoy the experience of living. You will learn to celebrate each moment and what a single hour can bring. Those around will join you in this celebration. Have you ever noticed how contagious seeing others celebrating is? Witnessing these moments of celebration, we are reminded of life being transient. Live the moment. You'll never know how many hearts you touch with your smile and positivity. You'll never know how changing the mood of people around you can make this place a better one. This way, you will find that the paradise you are looking for is not really a place but something hidden in your heart.

Remember

- Believe, even when you think there is nothing left to believe in.
- Practise faith daily and with firm devotion.
- Don't be influenced by other people's judgements and opinions.
- Accepting change and vulnerability will also loosen the grip of your ego on your soul.
- Only by surrendering to a higher power can you end your inner struggle.

Chapter 4

The law of humility

Humility is not thinking less of yourself. Humility is thinking about yourself less.

—Rick Warren

Soon after we moved into our new house, I was painting the outside walls when one of my neighbours approached me to ask about the colour. He wanted to be able to match it when the time came to painting his own pebble-dash. Matt was in his eighties, agile and alert, and, being an engineer by profession, he was still doing a lot of property maintenance in the area. I invited him inside, and we had a cup of coffee together.

After that first meeting, Matt and I met regularly, and we always had great conversations. I admired his zest for life and his simplicity. One day, I asked him, 'Matt, you look very content, you enjoy life, even the simplest thing brings a smile to your face. What is your secret?'

His face lit up, and he smiled and looked me straight in the eyes. 'Remember, Ben, you don't take anything with you when you leave this life. To live well, you need less than you think. Make every day count, and be curious about life. We are born to explore and to discover. To simplify your life, explore it first and discover what you value most. Then cherish everything.' He spoke with passion, and I could see that he was showing me his true self – a rare thing when so many people go around wearing a mask they never take off.

In our conversations, both Matt and I always showed our vulnerabilities and our real selves, speaking from the heart and expecting nothing in return.

'Shine your light in your daily interactions. Plant a seed of kindness in people's hearts and make this a daily habit,' he once told me. Not advice you hear every day. Matt was an inspiration to me, and I cherished our conversations and the time we spent together.

One Sunday morning, after a cup of tea in my garden, he stood up and said, 'Ben, my time is up. I'll go to Mass now, and in the afternoon, I will bring flowers to my wife's grave.' It was the last conversation we had. The following week, he departed to pastures new. I cherish his memory. Thank you, Matt, for your friendship and for your great advice.

The truth is that we, as human beings, tend to complicate things. We put enormous effort, and most of our time, into acquiring better positions on the social ladder, working tirelessly to get promoted or to expand our property portfolio only to find that inner peace has nothing to do with our worldly accomplishments.

When I made the decision to leave Romania, the country of my birth, I was searching for freedom from the tyranny of corruption. But even though I escaped, my soul was still imprisoned by the thirst for material things. It took me twenty-five years to realise that the only river that could satisfy my thirst was within reach, overflowing from my soul.

This reminds me of the story of the Acres of Diamonds. A farmer sold his land and everything he had so he could go in search of diamonds. He travelled far and wide, but no matter how deep he dug or how much effort he put into his quest, the rich reward of diamonds eluded him. Meanwhile, the man who bought his farm found something shining one day at the bottom of a stream crossing the land. It was a diamond. After searching some more, he found many others. The land the farmer had sold and left behind was full of the jewels he had not been able to recognise. The moral of the story is very simple: our treasure is closer than we think. If we are a bit more patient, and curious enough, we will find it.

When life delivered me a grave blow, and everything I possessed and had worked for crumbled in front of me, I entered the dark night of the soul. It took me a few years to recover, and I needed the help of some masters to build a new foundation for the life ahead. I have never looked back. My only regret is not seeing that light earlier, not discovering the diamonds in my own backyard. It is difficult to attain happiness when you are looking for it in all the wrong places.

Somehow, somewhere along the way, we have

picked up the idea that we need to fight for our joy. But this treasure is rooted already inside our hearts, far away from ambition and materialistic desires. When we complicate life, we bury our precious happiness, which should be allowed to sparkle like a diamond. So what must we do? We have to unlearn everything we know that blocks feelings of joy.

Every day, we are faced with hundreds of options. No surprise then that very often we make the wrong choice, and this usually develops into a bad habit. So, starting today, get rid of your unhealthy habits. Take small steps; keep it simple. Conquer your smallest dragon first: one small habit that you know is not good for you. Get rid of it and don't look back. Then, continue, continue, continue.

There are immense treasures to be discovered by living a simple life. When we moved into our new house, it was a great opportunity to make our lives simpler. With a blank canvas in front of us, we decided to declutter, starting with the furniture and the overall design of each part of the house. I built an outdoor kitchen with a transparent roof so we could cook outside. The patio, the walled garden with the vegetable plot and the hanging baskets became our favourite place to retreat no matter the weather. By slowing down, we begin to notice colours and wonders. We saw life with new eyes and gave our dreams a chance to catch up with us.

To live simply is to sail in the realm of the spirit. When anchored in a humble way of thinking and feeling, this sort of experience can bring you a type of joy that doesn't fade. We have to rediscover that *being* is our greatest gift. We should marvel at our existence: the present moment, in its uniqueness, is a place to behold.

We all come into this life with gifts, skills and talents, but somehow we only focus and develop those that help us to climb higher on the ladder of social status. Detachment from the compulsion to achieve goals, to acquire possessions, comes only when we follow God's plan for us: making every word and action an offering. Instead of surrounding ourselves with material possessions, we rely on our spirituality to reach our full potential. Simplicity allows us to develop new habits that help us progress on this spiritual path.

In May 2018, a friend of mine, Colm O'Brien, invited me to a meeting at the Professional Speaking Association Ireland, and I became a member the following month. That October, after a radio interview, when someone asked me to give a talk about 'Living on Light', I realised that the dream of being on a big stage, of speaking and doing presentations in front of thousands of people, was just another way of accumulating possessions and chasing wealth. Steadily, I was becoming the product of an inflated ego shouting loudly, 'Me, me, look at me!'

Fascinated by the lives of many saints, heroes and other wise men and women, I started to be curious by what made the difference between them and their contemporaries. There is a common thread, and this can be visible in any era of our human history. It was an unsurmountable upheaval, a big event that led their path to commit to a life of humility, simplicity and reverence. After the painful events of 2016–2017, I found myself in a dark cold place and very little help around. But I knew subconsciously that I was experiencing something dramatic that was sucking my life into itself. It was more than a change. It was an inner transformation that could be understood only in the quietude of my inner soul. Polished words and metaphors cannot explain it because it has to be experienced and not understood with the mind or the five senses. It is just beyond those things.

Luckily, my core mission of helping others did not change, and I started studying hypnotherapy. This became my new world stage: simply guiding others towards healing. I was still helping people, but in a humbler and quieter way and at a distance from the microphones, aeroplanes and flashy lifestyle. It was a decision that taught me a precious lesson: that we can follow a big dream and still remain humble in our faith.

Humility will help you achieve everything you

want, not by rising above anyone else but by remaining unattached to previous achievements. This is the paradox of humility: everything I have is mine but is not for my keeping. What I have is for sharing and for helping those I meet along the way.

With what I do, my seminars, my talks, my books and one-to-one clients, I have been told that I am helping numerous people. With the one-to-one clients at my hypnotherapy clinics in Dublin, I see the transformations in people, and my heart seems to flutter like a rainbow butterfly.

I get many messages of thanks, and I feel very humbled by what I read in these messages. These are happy moments. But when I look at myself in the mirror, I see an ordinary person: there is light and shadow and everything in between.

There is a saying, 'You cannot heal until you heal yourself,' and this is true. For example, I wanted to know why the wise masters emphasised the importance of fasting. I started to get into the habit of water-fasting every month. (Do not try this unless you are ready – and even then do it under supervision.) One day, I decided to do the programme called Living on Light, which extends for a period of twenty-one days. The first week, you don't eat or drink anything. The second week, you continue to abstain from solid food and drink only 25 per cent diluted fruit juice. The last week, you drink 40 per cent diluted fruit juice. It is not for everyone, and for this reason you need to check with your family doctor and a psychiatrist before beginning. But the mental clarity you reach can't be expressed through words or metaphors. Once you feel it, the words and clouds will evaporate. It almost cannot be expressed, but deep inside the heart, you taste … eternity. Now I do water-fasting each month for between three and eleven days, depending on my schedule.

When fasting, my mind becomes clearer and clearer. The humbleness overflowing from my heart chips away the pretences of a bloated ego. I also see at first hand the connection between the healing in myself and those knocking at the clinic's door, looking for advice and therapy. When I am water-fasting, the clients heal much quicker. The messages and the symbols received during the morning meditations reach a deafening clarity. I can feel the explosions of rainbows, butterflies and ecstasy expressed by the healed clients in my heart too.

Even today, feeling those silent moments that taste like honey in the mouth, I fall to the ground, filled with reverence and wondering, *Why me?* But why not! The fusion of my sufferings and the pure intentions directed towards the healing of other people is the key that opens many doors for me. I finally understand what the heroes, saints and masters were teaching: the darkness within hides so many treasures.

Nothing makes me better than you. I am trying to help others as much as I can while I am still learning to listen to and look for guidance. I take nothing for granted. I remind myself to stay grounded and not become a creation of others, to quiet my mind and to stay focused on my mission in this life.

Many clients come to the clinic complaining that

they feel misunderstood by their spouse, partner, colleagues or by their son or daughter. I can see their hurt. I always ask them a simple question: 'What about you? How well do you think you understand yourself?' Invariably, there is a deafening silence following my question, and I see the person in front of me struggling to find an answer. There is a good reason why I ask this question. To know and understand yourself requires a great deal of simplicity and humility. If we can't communicate and show our real self to others, it is because we haven't made contact with it in the first place. Are we afraid to discover our true selves? Is it the past we are trying to avoid?

Don't look back with regret. You cannot change the past; the present moment is all you have. It allows you to start anew. It requires a certain amount of courage, but mostly humility and simplicity.

Before you can teach others, first you have to learn. When you start every day with this reverence and humbleness in your heart, you realise that teaching and learning are part of the same thing: enhancing the experience of life. The most powerful way to live life to the fullest is to share whatever is in your heart. And the moment you manage to help one person, your life has meaning.

Humility is the key that opens the gate to a tremendous power rooted in your heart. It also gives you the opportunity to discover another dimension of your true self. Ask yourself, 'Who am I?' and 'Why am I here?' Every time you ask these questions sincerely, it is like peeling away all that is not essential in your life. When you do this, you go deeper and deeper until one day you realise that there is nothing out there that is not you. By remaining curious, there comes the feeling that you and God are very, very close.

At the Last Supper, in a supreme gesture of humility, Jesus offered to wash the feet of his followers. Likewise, embracing your life's mission and reaching the highest vision for your life requires not only courage but a great deal of humility.

An inflated ego creates turmoil inside, suffering and neurosis. This is like building a prison for ourselves, a cage that it's not easy to escape from. The selfish mind can neither understand nor master purity of spirit. It sees no sense in being humble or in planting seeds of change to bring a better harvest. You can show the mark of your wounds to others and still not shake their ignorance.

Blindness of spirit is a cross we humans bear. Maybe some people do not have the ability to understand revelations, even when looking at a miracle. Many of my clients who come to me looking for help, clarity or healing are eager to achieve what they are looking for as soon as possible. But recovery can be a slow process. You have to remain on course no matter what. Ask for help when you feel down. Remain humble but be proud of your steps towards healing. Only humility – not your intellectual abilities – can bring you there.

The outcome is beyond words: not being in conflict with anyone, being at peace with yourself and the world, you finally realise that the drama of the world has no longer any control over you. Every single day is a win-win situation. Every event you come across is a source of knowledge or of joy: either you win or you learn. People who are humble and have an attitude of reverence for life never stop learning and being amazed.

Many of us still live at the level of the ego-mind, seeing life as a war zone. If the only thing you nourish in life is the selfish 'me, me, me', everything that is not 'mine' is seen as an enemy and life becomes a battle. But when you live each day in a peaceful state of mind coming from deep within, the entanglement with yesterday's thoughts is dramatically reduced. The love overflowing from your heart envelops any sadness, isolation or drama.

Only inner peace makes us feel at one with the world around. Being humble is a threat to the egotistic mind, to the world as we experience it through our five senses. The gift of clarity of mind and inner peace is given to us only if we remain humble. It might seem counterintuitive, but being humble gives us tremendous power. We must use this power with pure intentions and release it only through love, trust and to help others.

The humble man or woman forgives and forgets. They help their fellow traveller. They console those who suffer, reassure those who doubt and encourage the one who's afraid.

But there's one thing you cannot do for your brother or sister: you cannot choose for them. The boundaries of each person's free will have to be respected. There is one person, and one person only, who is responsible for all your highs and lows, for all your tears and joys in life: yourself.

You can choose what to think, see and believe. Nobody can force you to do anything against your free will, not even God. God cannot choose for us; our free will has clear boundaries that will not be trespassed. And in order to know the best version of yourself, you need to become humble and live in simplicity.

Only those who want to follow and commit to this journey will receive this seed of change. You will become conscious of the radiant spiritual diamond that's already in your heart. Everybody possesses this diamond, but it is one thing to have it and quite a different thing to be aware of it and, most importantly of all, to let it sparkle.

Some people will not be able to grasp the meaning of life because they cannot understand something they have never fully experienced. If you were born without hearing, you would walk through life missing all the music and all the birds singing. For this reason, we have to forgive people who might not see things the way we see them. Forgive, before casting judgements or falling into the pride trap, thinking you are somehow better than someone else. Humility will help you to stay grounded and to realise that we are all on the same road to expand our lives and spirit, searching for unity and finding the divinity within.

You can be the most intelligent, charismatic person, but if you are not humble, you will never discover your true self. The key to your full unlimited energy, your full spiritual potential, is achieved only through humility. By remaining humble, you are granted access to a sixth dimension, one beyond the limitations of the senses. Once you feel it, it's almost impossible to describe it in words. It tastes like honey, like drops of pure grace. Any attempt to express this mystical feeling through words will distort that inner experience. It has to be felt first. This feeling will plant a seed that will start to germinate. Once the fragile roots find the perfect conditions inside the heart, you will feel at home.

So cherish your simple life. Being alive means that you already belong to a select club: you have the opportunity to remember, to be aware of the happiness within your heart. Focus on things you can change, like the way you look at things in front of you. Stop looking and comparing yourself to other people. Search for truth, and happiness will follow. Try your best to learn from whatever or whoever is in front of you. Start investigating every situation, especially the ones that create anger and irritation, and learn their lesson. Soon, you will find the treasure.

By remaining humble, we detach ourselves from the outside world, dramas, worries and troubles. Leaving the self-centred personality behind, we enter self-knowledge simply by choosing different thoughts, higher than our own thoughts. We start to see the world in a new light. We start dancing with life.

The key to being a source of healing and joy is to remain humble in our realisation: that we are in fact the source of what we see. We are creating the world around us, right now. You can change the world around you. Transformation is possible. Healing is achievable. Everything starts with choosing thoughts that radiate light and faith. So choose today, choose now. Keep knocking at the gates of your heart and release the diamond inside.

Remember

- Simplicity allows us to develop new habits that help us progress on this spiritual path.
- Everything you have is yours but is not for your

keeping. What you have is for sharing and helping those you meet along the way.

- The moment you manage to help one person, your life has meaning.
- Only inner peace makes us feel at one with the world around.
- To know the best version of yourself, you need to become humble and to live in simplicity.

Chapter 5

The law of clarity

The greatest beauty always lies in the greatest clarity.

—Gotthold Ephraim Lessing

Leaving your homeland to live in a foreign country can be a very daunting decision for anyone. But in 1991, I had to do it illegally, because of the East–West divide, and so the challenges were even greater. I was travelling without a visa and with just a basic grasp of Italian and a few words in German to communicate, passing through borders with real walls and real barbed wire, heavily guarded by soldiers with real weapons.

My parents and friends were genuinely concerned about my chances of surviving the journey. I never doubted. I knew I would be all right. My clarity of mind and purpose meant that I did not need to see the whole path in front of me. The flame of hope was enough to light up the path one step at a time. First one step, then the next, then the next … just bright enough to advance through my doubts, through my fears, through frozen rivers and pitch-black forests.

All I had to do was to hold on to that light and to keep walking. As the darkness cleared with the rising sun, if I just kept going, I was sure I would reach my destination.

Clarity of mind is like shining a light. Most of the time, the choices we make are not entirely our own, and we are not even aware of them. We choose what we choose, unconsciously, because everybody else made these same choices before us – or because our parents did – without giving much thought as to why and how.

Our minds are clouded by shadows of our past. It is the way we have been programmed. We accept, without questioning, beliefs and opinions that are not ours. We behave like clay figures being moulded by anyone who is powerful enough to manipulate us. We have forgotten that deep inside we carry the flame of immortality, shining like a precious diamond.

Instead of keeping the flame bright and the diamond shining clear, we let them become dull, suffocated by cheap, useless priorities. We follow the pack; we join the rat race. But is a diamond less valuable because it is covered in mud? When will we understand that we are already winners? That we are more than our eyes can see?

Clarity of mind is a state in which you are free from false beliefs and attachments. Your egotistic thoughts and emotions no longer control you. It is a prerequisite to enlightenment and to living a happy life. To have clarity of mind is to listen to the whispers coming from a realm deep within your soul. And this is possible only in … *silence.*

Being open-minded enables you to access a higher awareness, to get rid of past attachments, emotions and prejudices. To achieve this stage of clarity, you have to be willing to go deep into the dark castle of your former self, the rebellious person full of rage, to dismantle the illusions and heal the hurt: the hurt you inflicted on others and, most importantly, on yourself.

With humbleness in your heart, and the guidance of a master, you have to be willing to dedicate all your efforts to this journey of descent. Bit by bit, you will bring light to those frightening places you created. Fill them with light, light and more light.

When crisis forced me to reassess my entire life, clarity of mind was forced upon me. I am extremely grateful for the experience, but back then it felt like I was shouting for help in the middle of the night and I had lost my voice. Clarity helped me to steer away from despair and to focus on future possibilities rather than on present failures.

As part of my journey, I had to learn how to detach from old habits. They had become a hindrance for the new direction of our business: serving people. We kept all our businesses but downscaled the size of them and decluttered a lot of unnecessary expenses. So, immediately, we got more clarity through simplification without affecting the quality of the services, changing, learning and moving forward, despite not always seeing immediate progress.

My wife became more involved with the running of the crèches while I started the hypnotherapy course: education, healing and remaining in touch with our true nature and values. A perfect blend, I thought.

Trusting the inner path of the soul and the teachers we meet along our journey is part of never-ending process of re-creation and finding the answers hidden in our DNA, in our soul. It was one of my best clients, Brian F., who suggested that I put my name down for the School of Philosophy and Economic Science in Northumberland Road, Dublin 4. After finishing the first module, 'Wisdom', my teacher, Richard, came to me. 'I like the way you add something to the dialogue of this class,' he said. 'I would like to see you in the next module, which will explore clarity.' It is so refreshing to follow the advice of a master or teacher who sees potential and the divine spark in you.

With each new module, I explored and reached new depths and dimensions of my personality. I was unwrapping and polishing more faces of an unknown diamond inside my heart.

Before I knew it, I had been in the School of Philosophy for three years. My teachers introduced me to Transcendental Meditation. It took two years of my time and the courage to follow the advice of my masters. But isn't this the job of a true guide? To light the fire inside the student's heart so we can see our true potential in the splendour of the rainbow colours?

Meditation became a daily habit: thirty minutes at first, and after a few years an hour every day. The new practice of daily prayer and meditation started to unravel dimensions hidden inside my soul. Synchronising even more the mind, the body and the spirit, I started very clearly to follow the whispers I could hear in moments of deep silence. I became more present, and my attention was anchored deeply on what was in front of me.

I also started fasting, at first out of pure curiosity, starting with intermittent fasting, then pushing my body to the extreme, to the point of living on light. Towards the end of each period of water-fasting, my mental clarity increased dramatically. Having the inspiration and insight to detach from the accumulation of material things, the mission became diamond-clear, simplifying dramatically my life. Through all these practices, I gained clarity of mind, which helped me immensely and gave me direction and the ability to stay focused.

It is important to start correcting bad habits immediately. If not, your ability to manifest the best intentions will continue to be sabotaged by these hidden unconscious biases. When you start to listen to the voice of your soul, you will realise the immense potential you have and how this is unfolding in front of you, right *now*. Yes, this is a poetic way to describe it. You become a witness to the birth of a new person, but with the same soul. You look the same on the outside, but what has changed is the way you see the world, as if you are functioning with a different operating system.

And that's what will surprise those around you. Only those who've been in that place will fully understand what is going on. Spiritual clarity is not about having more: it is about lifting ourselves up by knocking down the barriers that have been erected around our selves.

To reach spiritual maturity, we need a quantum leap in understanding, to break the chains of material reliance. Wise people say that life is like a dream inside a dream until the moment you spiritually wake up. What you call your 'reality' is different from another person's reality. What *you* call 'my world' is nothing but a dynamic and ever-changing state of things, seen through your own senses and judged by your own mind.

In the final analysis, the most important thing is the decision about what world to create in your mind because this is exactly what you will witness next. In other words, we see every event that happens in this world not as it is but as we believe it to be. We add our own bias to it, so we see as we are. It is like our belief system, which our parents and society imprinted onto us and works like a pair of tinted glasses.

Because each of us has their own belief system, we see what we expect to see. There is always more to what we see with our own eyes, if only we have the inspiration to consider other alternatives, other realities beyond the veil of our senses. This explains why you can't see or fully understand your own immense beauty and contribution to the world.

Life, and the world you create, is like any other mirror. It reflects back whatever is in your mind. If you know and believe that to be true, then you are heading in the right direction. You become aware of your own power of seeing clearly what you are, where you are coming from and where you are going. If you do not like what you see, start again, and again, until you realise your infinite ability to become the best version of yourself. Try again, with a better understanding, with more humility and reverence for life and for others.

You are a creator: the creator of your own destiny. This is the greatest gift the universe gave you: the ability and the potential to create your new life the way you want it, simply by choosing what to focus on.

Therefore, it is important to know what type of thoughts you want to let in through your mental sieve. Thoughts, like seeds, if nurtured, have the potential to grow. What type of seeds do you want to plant? What is the crop you want to harvest?

Each one of us creates their own version of the world. A confused mind creates a confused reality. If you see only evil in people around you, that's exactly what you will create outside yourself in the world. Focusing on and entertaining only negative thoughts will lead eventually to a depressing environment. A barren, hostile landscape. Nothing grows there. How about choosing abundance? A rich and disciplined mind creates a reality where good seeds can grow.

Your thoughts are instruments. Are you using them to your advantage, to create more peace in your life, or are you using them to destroy the light of hope in your heart? As the Buddha said, 'Your mind is everything. What you think, you become.' The mind, with its unconscious habits and patterns, is running the show for you.

We are not fully aware of the power of the mind, but, if you can, imagine you are on a rescue mission and that this power is like a wireless transmitter and receiver. Used consciously and with reverence, to help others, it will bring about the rescue of those who are lost. It might even save lives. But if you refuse to use it, it serves no purpose whatsoever. It's just obsolete.

All of us are living in our own world, created by our own mind. We interpret things, we translate them in our own, unique language. When you look at me, you see me the way *you* believe I am. For this reason, I am not as I am but as you are because you look at me and 'understand' me in your own, unique way. So, you too are more than you think. For this reason, clarity will help you transcend the veil of doubts and procrastination. You do have a choice on where to channel your attention.

I think it is important to know how to 'waterproof' our minds in order to let in only thoughts that stimulate our growth and bring out the best in ourselves. When we are more preoccupied with negative events from the past or imagining a gloomy future, we lose our most precious gift, which is the present moment.

The greatest trap is living in a negative environment while lacking awareness of the present moment.

Another trap of negativity is continually comparing ourselves with others. During my seminars and speaking engagements, I meet people who tell me that they would like to follow the very same path as me. Not only is this not possible, they would not fully benefit from my own experiences. Why not? Because their own path is unique. Guidance is important, but the steps you take towards your dream are your steps and your steps only. No one can walk that path but yourself.

We are all here to accomplish a specific goal. Before your soul took on your body for this lifetime, you agreed to do a special and unique task. Engraved deep in your soul is the purpose you came here for. To fulfil that sacred promise means to be in synchronicity with your highest purpose. It means you have aligned your mind, body and spirit with your true calling, the highest vision for your life. Sometimes, along the way, we forget why we came. Clarity helps us to remember what we must become and do to remain in tune with that mission. Start serving others, and, before long, you will find your purpose.

The first step in being clear about what you want is to practise visualisation. After a while, when visualisation grows deep roots, you can move to a deeper layer of visualisation, which is visioning. The engine behind visualisation is imagination, and the engine behind visioning is intuition. In order to activate and ignite intuition, you will need on board pure intentions and a higher level of awareness.

To accelerate the transformation of the vision into reality, use one vital instrument: meditation. Beginning your visioning session with meditation is the doorway into an intimate closeness with a higher level of spirituality. By doing so, you are giving your consent to hear the imperceptible and see the invisible, achieving the impossible.

In those moments of deep transformation and simplifying my life, I repolished my mission statement: 'Service and healing, through detachment.'

Everything started to become clearer and clearer in my life. Yes, to reach a new level of mental stillness and calmness, a new way of thinking was needed. A new way of thinking that changed the way I was talking and brought a new way of acting, of attracting and manifesting miracles into my life.

So, how do you create your own mission statement that will bring you more clarity and concentration of your efforts in the direction of your desires? Nobody in this world knows you better than you know yourself. First, acknowledge that you have skills and qualities that the universe gifted you at the moment you came into this world. Make a list of your ten best talents and of activities that when you are doing them you lose track of time. When making the list, let your heart open and the words flow, without thinking about it too much. It's in you, and your heart knows what must be on that list.

Now look at the list again and from those ten choose the five strongest ones. Then reduce that further to three main qualities, the most relevant ones, the ones that will stand the test of resilience and time.

Imagine you are living in an ideal world, where money is not a problem. What type of service will you do with the qualities and skills you listed? Think about what activities you would love to do. It does not matter if you have to do a course to reach that destination. Just think in terms of what you love and would like to do for the rest of your life.

After you have found that, wrap those talents with a service you think you can lose track of time while doing. Then make a sentence starting with, 'My mission is to …' and add those qualities and talents directed towards others around you. The shorter your mission statement, the clearer your message will be.

You can travel to any place you want as long as you are fulfilling your mission. One mission, one life. The rest is just details. Follow your mission each day. Advancing whole-heartedly, you will also feel the dreams and your goal moving towards you.

Wouldn't you agree that to live and apply this simple principle of life requires a degree of humility and detachment from materialistic neurosis? It is exactly this humility and simplicity that will open your heart, bringing you clarity of mind and an invitation to live every day with more passion and intensity, as if everything that surrounds you is contributing to your spiritual blossoming. A life without clarity is like a ship sailing without a compass, but a clear mind and a vision give you the confidence to advance through the clouds of doubt and fears.

Count on your qualities and skills. Count on your mission statement and focus on your blessings. Your imagination and your vision will be guided towards the direction your heart aspires to. Your power is in your choice of thinking, speaking and taking action guided by the whisper coming from your heart. Trust and follow that whisper. Can't you hear it? Try again. It pierced my eardrums it was so deafening.

Your road reaches its fulfilment when you surrender completely. So stop looking at the world through a distorted lens and, instead, turn to the source. Allow God, the great truth of nature, or your own spiritual guides, to become the driving force of your own life, to infuse every thought, word and action with divine spirit. What follows can be described as an invasion of grace. Your life will be taken over, and clarity will result.

Becoming aware of the alignment between your mission and your soul gives you confidence that you are on the right path. It brings more clarity to the road into the unknown. It makes you realise that you are making progress on this 'pathless path', as Meister Eckart called it. The first step of that journey is to know where to start.

Many of us invest a great deal of energy in searching for clarity, often seeking it outside ourselves. Being eternally vigilant is a skill acquired through discipline, focus, prayer and meditation. For this reason, looking for clarity outside yourself brings you to a dead end. Seek it outside yourself, and you will not go far.

Blaming our failures on external events is to forget one simple truth. It is not God who is the source of our troubles, but ourselves. We sleepwalk into impossible situations and then look for cheap excuses.

Our habits and old beliefs act as blindfolds. For this reason, we have to make sure the intentions from our heart are pure and directed towards people asking for help. This way, our energy is guided towards a higher purpose, and, believe me, when you reach that point, Providence itself will look after minor details like paying the mortgage or making the ends meet.

To be aware of your soul is to be a silent witness of your personality. To feel the energy of your consciousness is to be aware of your own body, the way it reacts to everything, matter or feeling. The creative side of your personality goes hand in hand with your level of understanding. For this reason, a calm mind is vital in order to detach yourself from the world and become the driving force of your own life. It will allow you to get rid of the corrupt beliefs, convictions and habits that keep you grounded, making you their prisoner.

Once you are ready to let go, a chain reaction will produce a transformation beyond imagination. It will make you realise that everything in this life happens in order to awaken you so that you will remember who you really are. Once you wake up to the reality behind the veil of what you see, when you are awake spiritually, everything changes.

To have this gift is to see clearly, without attachments to old habits and beliefs. In fact, you discover a new dimension: you discover who you really are. You become aware of the ability to live at once in different dimensions. To reach that stage, the mind must be still and clear.

The more I learn from what is in front of me, the more my heart is tuned to my life's true purpose. Have you found yours? Becoming aware of the real self brings you closer to everything surrounding you, feeling a deep connection with every living thing. Sharing with others brings about extraordinary changes in your whole being. The landscape of your life changes instantly, starting with the removal of unconscious obstructions inherited from past generations. You start living your true potential not by accumulating more but by sharing what you have with those who you meet.

There are many talented people around us. But talent without preparation, discipline and action brings you nowhere. Begin today to sharpen those talents and skills and continue to develop them.

You spend so much of your mental and emotional energy on so many trivial things. Why not put it to good use and to your advantage? Start by having clarity inside your own being. This is the key to the door into wisdom of mind. Accessing and passing through that door means gaining a new kind of self-knowledge, based on self-analysis and self-observation.

Have the courage to question all that you have learnt so far, as if everything is built on foundations of sand. You will feel that the quest is just a drop of the infinite thirst for knowledge, but that humility will bring reverence and self-acceptance. This is the first step towards feeling and knowing divinity, which is beyond understanding but not beyond experience.

At some point, your physical strength will diminish – the body has limitations. But the mind has no limits. Your mind expands every time you share your gifts. What will keep you on top is the ability to think and prepare mentally. To be ready is to have a still and clear mind. To think is to create. Only a calm mind can find happiness in everything.

You will also realise that you can change the world only by observing it carefully. How? By becoming the very witness of your thinking, by being aware of every word that comes out of your mouth and every action you perform. You change yourself, and in that very instant the world around you changes by the simple act of observation. Infuse every thought, word and action with a divine vibration. Easier said than done, I know, but still worth trying.

When there is no clarity of mind, there is no clear path to choose, and there is a good chance that your ignorance will choose for you. So stop inviting trouble into your life. Leave behind yesterday's habits and choose wisely. It's like life itself is whispering softly in your ear: choose with pure intentions; choose from your heart. Have the courage to follow your heart. There are treasures inside.

Remember

- Most of the time, our choices, beliefs and opinions are not our own, and we are not even aware of it.
- Clarity is a state in which you are free from false beliefs and attachments.
- Clarity is a prerequisite to enlightenment and to living a happy life.
- Each one of us creates their own version of the world.
- Focusing on negative thoughts will create a depressing environment.
- We see every event that happens in this world not as it is but as we believe it to be.
- A life without clarity is like a ship sailing without a compass.

Chapter 6

The law of love

Love is the whole thing. We are only pieces.

—Rumi

They say, 'Be careful what you wish for,' and it's true. In the space of four years, I changed career, wrote and published a successful book and co-wrote a second one while also expanding my businesses. I felt then that the time was right for my family to move house – yet another dream to focus on and one that charged my days with positivity, purpose and excitement.

There was a hidden price to pay, however, for moving into a new area. For reasons known only to him, our neighbour did not seem to like us very much. We were quiet, discreet and as friendly as possible, but we were met with hostility.

Most people would have moved immediately. Did it deter me from enjoying life in the new place? No. I sensed suffering in his life, so I knew I had to be as patient as possible. The builder, the engineers and the architect all advised me to go to the police and report his behaviour. Instead, I went not where most people suggested I go, but into a church. Was there a lesson for me to learn from my neighbour? If so, what was that lesson? I kept asking and asking, and eventually, while spending time in silent meditation, the thought of Gandhi came to me. Gandhi once said, 'You cannot change the world, but you can change yourself.' And so, I started praying for our next-door neighbour, for his wife and for his son. I prayed sincerely, wishing them all blessings and peace in their lives. I continued to pray and to meditate every morning, and, while I did, I imagined enveloping all our neighbours in spiritual protective armour, showering them with as much love, forgiveness and perfect health as I could.

This decision seemed to turn the tide dramatically in our favour and to improve the dynamic of my relationship with my neighbour, his family and the whole neighbourhood. The situation taught me to be patient and to give generously without expecting anything in return, a life lesson that I am grateful for.

We all react differently in the face of adversity.

How would you feel if you discovered that your child would be incapacitated for the rest of their life? This is a suffering beyond words, and no doubt it takes a heavy toll on your mental health. In difficulties, many people break down, unable to find answers to their problems. In the middle of the storm, it is difficult to imagine that life has other plans and better things in store, but believe me, this is true most of the time, if we could only find a bit of faith in our hearts.

Begin each day with compassion in mind. As soon as you wake up, remember Buddha's teaching: the importance of kindness and compassion. In the Buddhist tradition, compassion and love are seen as two aspects of same thing: compassion is the wish for another being to be free from suffering; love is wanting them to have happiness. Wish love and something good for others, even to those neighbours and co-workers who fail to understand or appreciate you.

We are all interconnected and want the same for ourselves and our families. So, make sure the intentions for others, coming from your heart, are infused by love's radiating light. One efficient way to cultivate compassion is mindfulness, the process of bringing one's attention to experiences occurring in the present moment. Mindfulness develops the ability to recognise distress in ourselves while encouraging emotional balance in the face of adversity.

Another way you can actively show compassion to others is to donate your time to a worthwhile cause. Volunteering implies hope and is a way to reach out and use your skills to improve the lives of others.

Compassion is a two-way street. Having compassion for people around you will change their hearts. But when you treat yourself and others *without* love and compassion, you go against the heart, against your true nature, and this marks the beginning of suffering. You will spread that suffering wherever you go. Every action, word and thought of yours will be motivated by fear and the desire to control.

Control is the biggest mental lie you will encounter. It's an illusion created by your self-interest. This state of mind will isolate you more and more. An inflated ego is never happy with assuming a humble position in this puzzle. The ego needs a pedestal and control. The opposite of this road is the highway of vulnerability and love.

When you find the middle path, the heart knows that you are part of the tapestry of life. You begin to forgive even those who made you suffer, finally understanding that the aggressors are going through life half asleep, harming themselves and others. Help them if you can. Actively listen and offer help, especially if someone needs it. Be fully present. Put any distractions away and give your full attention to what is being said. Listening provides relief to those in a world that can be indifferent to suffering. Do not interrupt the person speaking and check in on them at a later time to reinforce the knowledge that you were truly listening.

In the very act of liberating them, they are also transformed, like the blind man seeing clearly for the first time. You begin to understand that there is no division between the created and the creator. Not being tormented by the past anymore, the healed person is transformed from being a drop in the river into becoming a source of light. You become the master of a new destiny. By synchronising your life's purpose with the divine dance of the great ocean, you are breaking the chains of fate. You have finally arrived home. Wherever you go, love, healing and compassion overflow from the heart.

There is nothing you can fully control in this life. For this reason, it is imperative to keep a harmonious relationship with everything that surrounds you. How does it feel to be in the middle of that harmony? When you live with compassion, you seek no control. Your heart opens, and love flows like a nectar through you and those around. Everything operates differently as the foundation of your actions is now built on transparency, on love, on divine contemplation and a deep reverence for life. You are not dazzled any longer by anything that glitters, material riches, pride or recognition. You rise higher and higher from the bottom of the ditch.

The world offers us many opportunities to observe

the beauty and the miracle of life. By witnessing tender moments of kindness, generosity and love, our heart beats faster, recognising the magic of the moment. If there is no love in your heart, you would not be able to notice it. As simple as that. It hurts when we witness injustice and persecution. It hurts seeing anything restricting freedom, truth and beauty. This is a clear sign that we are in a relationship with everything that surrounds us. When you are down, just look inside your heart. Appreciate the fact that you are alive, and nothing is lost if you decide to continue the journey. This is a great starting point. Can you feel your legs, your arms? Can you see your smile in the mirror? You are already a winner. It's so easy to forget and not to realise how lucky you are. Count your blessings, my friend.

There are two ways to learn in this life: you can learn with love, or you can learn with pain. It is not easy when suffering takes over and you are losing your voice shouting for help. For many people, these moments of pain and anguish feel like the end of the world. I walked that very thin line myself in the autumn of 2016 until the summer of 2017. The desperation was so intense, it felt like the hands of time had stopped, with me frozen and trapped inside that agony.

Taking responsibility meant that I stopped pointing the finger. I stopped blaming other people or events outside of my control. When I did that, the clouds lifted from my mind and clarity enveloped my heart. I saw the world with new eyes, and the only thing I could say was, 'How could I have been so blind?' The seeds of that vision were planted during the motivational speaker event at the Convention Centre in Dublin, in January 2017, and culminated with a retreat in Florence, Italy, led by Jack Canfield, renowned motivational speaker and author of *Chicken Soup for the Soul*.

It took me about eight months to get out of my cave and follow my new vision. I didn't do it alone. It was Jack who encouraged me to keep going, telling me that I was ready. He gave me the push I needed. Without hesitation, I jumped into the unknown, over the threshold of fear and a doubting heart. I was not 100 per cent convinced, but I jumped. I was not ready, but I let go of my past anyway.

What followed shook my entire belief system to the core. Where I was expecting to fall, I discovered I was soaring higher and higher. Going into the unknown, I got my life back. I would have arrived at this point so much more quickly if I had had a teacher to follow from the very beginning.

A true guide won't try to teach you every single thing you need to know. They are there just to give a glimpse of your true potential, to show you how to become free from the bondage of fear and past conditioning. That ability is already built in your DNA, but it needs to be rediscovered. The qualities you see in your teacher are qualities you also have, otherwise you wouldn't be able to recognise them. They are present beside you only temporarily, holding your hand for a while, until you can see the possibilities that lie ahead. They are there to guide you towards that incredible vision, treasure and potential that might be covered by the ruins of a broken heart.

Your teacher or master is not *better* than you. They are just ahead of you on the path, and only because they started their journey a bit earlier than you are starting yours. Eventually, you become your own master.

By meeting my teacher, my eyes began to open. My awareness changed, and I became extremely focused and filled with positive energy. It was the start of a healing journey. The following steps showed me that there was no escape from this vision. Embracing it was the only option. This is the point where I became my real self, where I consciously recreated, embraced and accepted the multidimensional me. This is the mark of real success, the beginning of what the wise philosophers were preaching: 'Know yourself.'

Sharing your gifts or blessings is a sure way to fight against this oppression of spirit. Life is there to be lived, shared and enjoyed. For this reason, it is good to keep your intentions clear, to let the blessings of your life flow freely, by sharing your gifts with the world. You attract light, abundance and love by sharing and not by holding on, and this will make all your actions more meaningful. Do not hide your skills and your gifts from others. The universe gave you those gifts out of love and compassion, for sharing and not for your desire to control and possess more. Keeping them hidden transforms them into a powerful tyrant, and you are the first victim.

If you want to understand the world, take a close look at the mystery of relationships. We are all connected with everybody and everything all around us. First, watch the interaction between you and everything around you. Be present and curious by observing your own actions and thoughts. Listen to your own words and become aware of their impact on everything. By going and looking inside, you will see the world in a new light. You will realise that the heart is the nest of your soul and has one main purpose: to keep expanding and growing through vulnerability and love.

What do we do instead? We seek to control the world and life itself by building walls around us, chasing pleasures and craving security. But your soul, believe it or not, loves vulnerability. The reason is that to love is to become vulnerable: to be seen as you really are. That's bravery.

The heart operates differently from the logic of the mind. This is true. By connecting to the heart of another person, you are stepping into another world. This is the ideal ground for love and compassion to grow, to bloom and spread its fragrance over the world. It is not until you have the patience, curiosity and vulnerability to listen to what another person has to say, that you make a giant leap into love and compassion. By doing that, you are given the key to access a new dimension of life, where everyone is more than its individual parts. By engaging in that kind of relationship with your neighbour, with your brother and sister, you are seeing the world with new eyes, as if you are given the password combination to open the door to a new reality. This is the real power. Standing at the threshold between humanity and divinity, love and compassion flowing from your heart, you bow low so others can feel at home. This marks the transition from human level into spiritual level.

Love's boundaries are so subtle. When you hold on to someone too tight, two things could happen: you might suffocate them, taking away their freedom, or you will slowly but surely lose your sanity, trying to control everything. The desire to possess what you love creates a lot of suffering. This kind of relationship slips very soon into manipulation. Imagine that you enjoy the company of a delicate bird. You would hold it gently in your open palms. If it flies, the bird was never yours. If it returns to you, just smile.

People start romantic and loving relationships expecting them to last forever. I have seen it so many times in my clinic: two people who started a beautiful journey together less than one year ago are now desperate to save their relationship or their marriage.

Relationships are all about sharing. Close relationships have many ups and downs and require effort. Life is complicated. Keeping the freshness of the relationship takes hard work. It needs a conscious effort from both parties. Why? It is because a relationship will test your limits like nothing you've encountered before. True intimacy has nothing to do with what you expect to get in return but with what you are ready to give without reservations, which is everything.

Likewise, an egotistic mind will force its view on others. We do it ourselves to a certain degree when we refuse a different point of view just because we think we know better. This is exactly why relationships in business, work and family are sometimes so painful. It is because of our expectations, desires and demands. You want people to act the way you want them to act. Once you give up these expectations, you will experience great joy and relief from suffering.

If you are really interested in solutions, you would go deeper and try to understand why you reacted this way. The moment you realise that the person in front of you might have a different point of view and that you don't need to control it, that, my friend, will be the end of your illusions of selfish grandeur. At the same time, it marks the end of your suffering. The first step towards healing starts with accepting others as they are.

The reality is – and life shows it in abundance, every single day – that the path to joy and happiness never was, never is and will never be through the approval and acceptance by society. As belonging needs approval, this contradiction can bring frustration and suffering. A clear mind will recognise belonging and approval for what they are: balance and fairness. Belonging and acceptance on terms that are not in alignment with your moral values will create tensions and turmoil. Acceptance forced upon you only brings unhappiness. What kind of acceptance is it when you are not allowed to write your own story?

I see it every day with my clients at the clinic. Our peace of mind is constantly undermined by our lack of patience and by our being consumed by desire. We think the grass is greener on the other side, but this is all in the mind. We are all in the same boat. How do you know the other person is better off than you? Is it because they are driving a better car, or have a holiday home? You are fooling yourself. Accepting others without fear means letting go of your judgements and prejudices. This alone will open a new dimension inside your mind. This will give you a tremendous amount of freedom and self-confidence. Your understanding of life will be exponentially enhanced. By loving more, the reverence for life starts to grow deeper roots. The more you understand, the more you love. The more you love, the more you understand.

Your vision will become clear when you surrender completely and follow the chosen path. It is a total commitment, and yet there are no guarantees that you will reach a specific destination. It is a journey of many layers. The more you advance in that multidimensional journey and into your vision, the more you will remember. The more you remember, the thirstier you will get to know more.

You create the best life by stepping into the current, that stream that carries you further and further. By stepping into that picture, you become the main actor of that vision. The courage to embrace and stay with that vision is the vehicle that brings you one step closer to the destination. Once you feel that presence inside the heart, you understand without seeing. You don't need proof anymore. Your soul begins to create whatever you desire in order to help those around you – but never for your own benefit. This is the key: put everything to the benefit and healing of those asking for help.

Being in alignment with your vision, you become a living magnet, attracting positivity. And creating positivity becomes a joy. Because you are in tune with creation, the past and the future become concentrated into the present moment. You realise that this life is the greatest show on Earth. Like a dream inside a dream. The paradox of this show is that the more you enjoy it, the more you become detached from it. Detachment is the other key ingredient in fully enjoying this life.

Having the courage to embrace your life's purpose, your vision, is not easy. It takes courage and sacrifice. But once you have a glimpse of the possibilities ahead, you realise that the alternative is living a life of anxiety, depression and mental turmoil. By having courage, faith and humility in accepting your vulnerability, your whole being is open to possibilities, permeable and capable of being changed into something more – something better, as if 1 + 1 is not 2 anymore but 11. The mathematics of divinity is more miraculous than what we learnt in school. For this reason, the universe is a thousand times more ready to give than we are ready to receive.

We are obsessed with safety and power, but the real world is all about change and vulnerability. When you are ready and curious to explore the hidden dimension, the place where love and compassion come from, you will know the meaning of real power. It can be embraced only when you accept your vulnerability. We have to see failures as opportunities to awaken the soul. Obstacles make us aware of a hidden dimension behind suffering. That's where love and compassion come from.

Life needs spirituality, love and light. By living in love and immersed in light, you develop a sense of belonging and synchronicity with the universe. Finally, you understand that life has always been on your side. It's like the entire universe has been guiding you towards this moment of awakening. You are not tormented any longer by divisions and conflicts. By choosing the path less travelled, which is the path of compassion, you discover that where love is, there are also miracles.

Your heart, now full of love, will experience a quantum leap in understanding, realising that every second of suffering you've been through had a purpose: to awaken divine possibilities. Free of contradictions and with a clear mind, you answer positively the invitation of being part of something bigger than life itself. You become part of a divine dance and know that this short life is just preparing you for something much greater. Whatever you want for the greater good will become reality.

Life is complex, and it is not always about finding yourself through someone who can love you. Many people think that only in a relationship will they feel fully alive. For some, this may not be the case. For many, life's journey is about finding their own selves. It's about knocking at the heart's gate until it opens. What are you going to find inside? Only doubts and suffering? Look the pain and the hurt straight in the eyes. And when all the barriers are down, have the courage to dance and laugh until you get dizzy. Love yourself and love others. Remain curious about life even when you are hurt. Go all the way. Even a broken heart hides so many diamonds.

Remember

- Begin each day with compassion in mind.
- When you live with compassion, you seek no control.
- There is no division between the created and the creator.
- Life is there to be lived, shared and enjoyed.
- We are all connected with everybody and everything all around us.
- Relationships are all about sharing.

Chapter 7

The law of prayer and meditation

The value of persistent prayer is not that God will hear us, but that we will finally hear God.

—William McGill

It was Jack Canfield who introduced meditation to me, at the retreat in Florence in 2017. Before the retreat, Jack asked each of us attending to write down a list of five dreams we wanted to achieve and to bring it with us. My dreams were: (1) Write a book and sell 1 million copies. (2) Become an international motivational speaker. (3) Double the number of crèches by the end of 2018. (4) Build a retirement home in my village in Romania, as a thank-you to my community, teachers and masters. (5) Buy my daughter, Julia, a dog.

(You might be laughing, but because my wife, Vasi, loves having the house in a pristine state, this last dream proved to be a very difficult one.)

At one of our daily meetings, Jack asked me, 'How long will it take you to fulfil the dreams on your list?'

'Ten years,' I replied, full of optimism.

He continued calmly. 'Do you pray?'

'Yes,' I said, rather timidly, not knowing where the conversation would go.

'How would you feel, Ben, if I told you right now that everything on your list can be achieved in half the time? But in order to accomplish that, you will have to meditate every day – especially after you pray. The prayers are working, but try to meditate in silence after finishing your prayers. We will teach you how to do that here, and you can carry on with this daily practice. If you do that, you will achieve your dreams in five years.'

I started to smile, not knowing if he was joking. My list of dreams was rather extensive, and the idea of achieving all that in only five years left me perplexed. In the meantime, he repeated, 'Just by meditating … and, Ben, I will buy ten copies of your book, even before you publish it.'

I could not hide the amazement from my face. We both started to laugh, and something really special and magic, like a divine grace, enveloped that moment.

'As simple as that, Ben. You had better believe it.'

I trusted my teacher, a very special man. When I came back from Tuscany, I started getting up every morning at 3.33 in the morning. No messing. No jokes. I was curious to find out why Jesus and many saints, spiritual masters and even scientists had meditated at this same hour, before the sun was up. I wanted to see how far I could go and, most importantly, what could be achieved when total faith in a master was supported by a gladiator-like discipline and resilience.

The practice of meditation and contemplation brought to me wonderful fruits and a new, rewired mind. After a while, each new morning felt like a fresh beginning, and this helped me to start each day with a sense of wonder, like going into a magnificent unexplored territory. I also started to leave behind bad habits.

Why is it important to learn to pray or meditate? Prayer and meditation teach you to focus: to clear your thoughts and to stay detached from the noisiness of the mind. By not listening to every thought that comes up, you focus only on what matters most, leaving all the unwanted luggage behind. One fifteen-minute session of morning meditation sets up solid stepping stones for the day and a positive mood to face whatever may come your way. You start looking at the day ahead from a different perspective. And at the end of that day, you get to look back filled with satisfaction because, whatever happened, you did your best. When the next morning comes, you start all over again, but without any expectations upon yourself or the day – as if starting for the first time. This way, every moment is new and fresh, without the memory or burden of yesterday.

Generally, praying requires you to say or read some verses from memory or a book. This will create a vibration in your mouth and in your head. With devotion and regular practice, this can lead to a deep state of contemplation and a melting into God, or Jesus, or a specific saint, until you forget about time and yourself. Meditation requires a deep silence and stillness of mental activity. Your external stillness reflects the interior calm and tranquillity. With practice and patience, you can reach altered states of consciousness that you could never have imagined before you took to this habit.

So why do we pray and meditate? We do so because we feel we are more that the eyes can see. We feel in our hearts a hidden potential ready to be explored and realised.

While in a meditative state or praying, thoughts and distractions may come your way. Let them come and go. Do not get attached by your discursive mind or ego's false pretences. Repetition and discipline will purify your mind and heart, simplifying your life. Repeating a specific mantra or words will bring you into a deeper silence, and at a certain point in your practice you will realise that the whole universe is in you and not the other way around. You feel that God is the truth, that God is within you. And there is never a barrier between the truth and the man. In this higher level of consciousness and awareness, you can transcend the limitations of your physical boundaries.

Through praying and meditation, you can develop the faculty of listening to the whispers of the universe, or to the Higher Self coming from a realm above our capacity of understanding or trying to describe it with words. But following that whisper requires courage and humility as well. It is this humility that embraces the heart and mind together and brings to us the greatest mystery: *ourselves* – a mystery that can be felt only by surrendering to love and humility. Only in this love can the energy of God/Christ/Buddha take and transform us beyond ourselves and the mystery of existence. So, our awakening is not into God, because we are divine already. Our awakening is into man. As Saint Athanasius said, 'God became man so man may become God.'

It is important to set the tone for the day by meditating or praying very early in the morning. It's not easy, but once you get into the discipline of rising before anyone else, let's say between 3.30 and 4 a.m., by the time the rest of the world is up it feels like you are already a thousand miles ahead – even though you are not in a competition with anyone, of course. Getting up from your bed early gives you a chance to quiet down, to listen, to prepare and to pay attention throughout the day. The rest will follow.

Prayer and meditation help you to achieve a state of awareness. And when you are truly aware you see things differently. You have a new perspective, a clearer image of yourself. In the silence of your meditation, you are better able to tell your unique song apart from the myriad of other sounds that fill the air. And when you follow that inner voice, you discover your true nature.

During meditation and contemplation, once you reach a certain level of calm and stillness, the perception of time dissipates, and your mind is drawn towards the vast calm lake of consciousness. The joy in your heart is beyond words.

You will, no doubt, be transformed by the experience. That transformation should bring a sense of unity and belonging. You will feel content and at peace with everything.

Many times, this feeling envelops me while coming from a long day at work, and I find myself thanking the universe for the day of service and for keeping me safe. I feel a total communion with nature. This feeling gives me the confidence to do more and to look with optimism to tomorrow.

I have been asked, ‘How do I recognise this feeling of unity? What is it like?’ It is different for everyone. It will be different for you. Sometimes, there are tears of happiness, and waves of calmness flood your heart. You are not thinking anymore as a separate entity, and everything is just a deep, profound experience. It will last for a split second at the beginning, and you will definitely know when it’s gone. Try not to run after that moment. Do not chase it. The more you attempt to recreate it artificially, the more disappointed you will feel. Just enjoy it when it happens. With practice and devotion, it will come.

The nature of the mind is to produce thoughts all the time. And once we allow our minds to get distracted, we go off course. In the middle of your meditation, your subconscious will bring up thoughts that have nothing to do with what you had in mind when you started the exercise. Things to do, things left undone … Like a monkey swinging from branch to branch, your thoughts will jump from one topic to another. In seconds you can be a thousand miles away from your first thought. Imagine talking to a friend, face to face, only to realise that your friend is not really listening. How would you feel about that? This always happens when our doubts and fears are still strong.

I cannot emphasise enough the importance of being in the present. This means being 100 per cent attentive to what is in front of you right now, and it is also a way to anchor yourself. While you were washing your face this morning, maybe you were thinking and planning the day ahead. Next time, instead, when looking in the mirror, acknowledge the simple fact that it feels good to be alive. Look at life as a miracle.

Practise this habit, and before long your life will feel different.

Deep listening is the heartbeat of meditation. When you find yourself facing a problem, not knowing what to do next, try to imagine how some great spiritual person would have approached thc problem. Ask yourself, 'What would they do in my place, in this situation?' Then, just listen. The answer will come in a form only you will understand. Be quiet, listen attentively and follow that answer through.

You will be surprised, but, in this state of mind, good things will begin to happen in your life. You will attract positive energies, and the moment you need something solved, the solution will manifest itself faster than you think.

The most important thing, though, is the joy that envelops you, knowing that the heart is the seat of your soul. Other rewards are just a bonus, and you must not obsess over that flow of joy. Just keep still and live in the present. Effort, discipline, wisdom, patience and pure intention are all essential.

Keep going today as far as you can go. Keep going until there is no road left in front of you. Weed out any negative thought the moment you become aware of it. If not, negativity will drag you deep into the mire of depression. Each one of us has accumulated tensions and conflicts along the way, and there is always a battle inside, no matter how good life feels in the present moment. Detach yourself from this mental neurosis.

Don't worry if you cannot see the solutions to your problems in life. You are more than your worries and your thoughts about tomorrow. Your job is to allow everything that is good in your life to germinate, grow and bloom. It is up to *you* to break the chain of negative thoughts and to become a witness to positivity.

At some point or points, life will present you with an opportunity in one form or another. Experience has shown me that very few people answer this call or take this opportunity when it comes knocking. Why? Is it because they think they can do it all on their own? Are they too proud to ask for help? There can only be one answer.

What is your answer? What stops *you* from being your real self, from living on your own terms but in harmony and at peace with everything around you?

Why are people afraid of making big, important decisions, even though they can see the present situation is truly unbearable? They see that change is needed; they know that they need to answer a call; but it seems to me that there is simply too much mental noise in their life, and it's no surprise they can't hear anything – let alone the soft whisper of their heart.

I remember one time a client shared his plans for the future with me. At each subsequent session, I was ready to congratulate him, to embrace him and to wish him well. The plan, the future, even the details, they all made perfect sense. He had only to prepare himself, to gather enough momentum and to start on this new journey. What I wanted to hear from him were these words: 'I am ready.' Suffice to say, I never heard those words.

We have to accept that some people will fall short of their own expectations, and there's not much we can do about it. Those decisions are theirs and theirs alone. No one will make these big decisions in life for you.

It doesn't really matter if you were born here or there, if you were born rich or poor. Once you hear the voice of intuition coming from the heart, and then take action, the duality and the battles inside begin to evaporate. You experience more unity, and you experience a sense of surrender and peace. The inner and outer dimensions will begin to synchronise harmoniously.

So put all your efforts to self-improvement and to raising your awareness. This way you will know that there is no such a thing as 'Destiny' imposed by God or the gods upon you. What you call destiny is just yesterday's habits acting upon your self. When you understand this, you realise that your awareness becomes the measuring tape of what you create and consider to be real.

You have total freedom to do what you want today, and that will have an impact on your tomorrows.

When you are on track, focusing on your future goals will keep away the frustration of daily defeats and negativity. Don't think of the harvest yet. *You* are the harvest, with branches bending under the weight of good fruit. *You* are the path. Just listen to and follow the whispers of your heart. The rest is just details.

Your mission is to guard the treasure within your soul. Do not be concerned about your spiritual progress. You are part of life, and everything you create has value, even if you do not see it immediately.

Prayer and meditation help you to see and hear with your heart. By practising them, you create the right conditions to open a window, an internal ear, into your heart so you can listen to and learn to trust the voice of your intuition. Once you start praying with sincerity and humility, you can make every single moment on Earth a little paradise.

We are here on Earth to create and experience a state of joy. This is our universal call. It can be a lifelong adventure to arrive at your destination. If you are wise, you will follow a teacher or master, someone who has walked the path before you, to guide you through the process and to help you arrive at your destination more quickly.

The presence of a teacher can save you a lot of time, energy and money. They will give direction and motivation. So find a master. Stick with them and have the vulnerability to let yourself be modelled by their wisdom. You will find that old veils of ignorance are lifted for good. You will begin life again on a fresh path, and the clarity of your thoughts, words and actions will multiply.

What will this new path look like? It could mean getting rid of bad habits or bettering yourself by starting an educational course, educating yourself in a field where you can shine. It could mean a change of career, or leaving behind something that gives you no joy. These are changes that lead to new places, to heights from where you will see things in a brighter light and give birth to a new, better self, creating a brighter future and shaping your life as you see fit. And when you arrive at your destination, remember where you came from and try to help others who are stuck to change course. Stay humble.

Meditation is fascinating because you never know where it will bring you. If you want to commit to a practice, have faith and be humble but, most importantly, persevere. Keep the focus and the momentum you need to make progress. Take small steps, one day at a time.

The moment you think you have made some progress, you might realise that everything is not as you wished, that there are still battles to be fought. You might grow frustrated and, instead of feeling at peace, feel disappointed. At this point, your decision to continue or to give up will most likely define the rest of your life. With focus, you can guide your mind's attention to the present. You can regain stability and a new awareness by which you can truly see the beauty of life and all that you can embrace today.

Any person can reach a higher level of consciousness through the practice of meditation. Something extraordinary happens when the mind declutters, relaxes and does not follow the thoughts that come and go like clouds in a blue sky, when you experience pure contemplation. When you start your day from that new foundation, unattached to old habits, you feel truly safe because everything you experience is love. So be still, do not be bothered by the rising thoughts, and come back to a focal point: a word or an image that can keep you still and quiet. By going back to that point, you knock at the gate of a new dimension. It's up to you to open that gate.

So, why not start this practice today? For the next sixty-six days, wake up thirty-three minutes earlier than you have to and pray, in your own way. You might want to pray for something very specific, but pray as if you've already achieved what you wanted. See your dream already manifested. Get in touch with that high vibration that makes your heart celebrate. Do not say 'Give me' or 'I want', but instead say, 'Thank you for making my dream a reality.' Have a try. The results are from another world.

Remember

- If you want to achieve your most impossible dreams, even in half the time you planned, start meditating today.
- Prayer and meditation teach us awareness and focus and to stay detached from the noisiness of the mind.
- When you meditate regularly, you see things differently.
- Join a group or find a teacher who resonates with you, and follow their guidance.

Chapter 8

The law of gratitude

The more grateful I am, the more beauty I see.

—Mary Davis

In June 1991, just two days after completing my final university exam, I made the decision to emigrate – to leave behind not only my country, my family and my friends but also my roots and my history. At the time, I felt I was answering a call that was coming straight from my heart. I had many questions and very few answers about the road ahead of me, about decisions I would have to make. I was young and maybe not wise enough to fully understand how life really worked. But deep inside my heart I knew that if I waited to find the answers to my questions, I would miss the chance to build my own future.

I did not look back.

Those who have taken the path before you will tell you that the way reveals itself in its own unique fashion and that once you see it you will recognise it. In the depths of your being, you will know that there is no other alternative. You will surrender. By trusting your heart, you stop searching for proof, and you follow your dream.

I heard a story many years ago about a boy who had to travel a couple of miles to deliver something for his father. It was dark already, almost night, and the boy realised that he would have to walk the whole distance with only a small torch to light his way. He looked down at the torch in his hand and almost lost courage, not knowing how he would find his way through the night with a torch that could only light up the road for three feet ahead. A wise man passing by saw the young man's hesitation, his fears and doubts about walking in the dark. The man pointed out that with each step the light would also move forward, and that it would *always* light up three feet ahead of him so the boy should not be worried just continue to walk. The boy did just that, and he reached his destination.

When you have big dreams and long-range goals, like I did when I left my country, one thing that can keep fear and frustration at bay is the simple practice of gratitude. Having a sense of gratitude acts like the boy's torch. It lights the path ahead of you and lets you see what's right in front of you. When you are grateful, you become more present and focused not on what you lack but on what you already have.

A lack of gratitude, on the other hand, will make your path more difficult to follow. Having no light to guide you means that you will be afraid to become what you are meant to be. During the most difficult times in my life, that gloom kept me chained as if imprisoned at the bottom of a dark cave.

But we can displace all that negativity with an attitude of gratitude. Gratitude keeps your attention focused on the gifts in your life instead of allowing you to fall into the trap of despair. Whatever we refuse to feed eventually shrinks and dies. Soon, there is nothing left but crumbs of memory, and we are free to move on and live fully.

Even in times of deep distress and hardship, it is always possible to be grateful. It took me over twenty years to grasp the concept that although it is difficult to change your environment, you can always change your thoughts. By doing so, you create a ripple effect that can lead to total transformation. When I was experiencing my dark night of the soul, I learnt to put everything into perspective and to see things differently. I counted my blessings, starting with the miracle of being alive. After all, once you are alive and kicking, you can still achieve a lot. Remembering this simple truth kept me going and gave me courage to regroup and refocus my skills and talents. Saying 'thank you' for just being alive is like being in love with painting and having a new canvas every single day that you can paint just the way you want. The rainbow is your limit.

This is today, and who knows what tomorrow will bring? So better make the most of it now. Start creating your masterpiece today.

Gratitude is the most powerful habit you can cultivate, and if you practise it daily, it will change your life. A grateful person doesn't raise their fists towards the sky. They navigate through life peacefully and are ready to deal with whatever life has to offer. They may have a plan of action, but the plan is flexible, and they usually put others first – even before themselves.

A grateful heart finds happiness in the smallest things. I remember once walking into a local bakery, and at the back of the shop I saw wooden shelves stacked with freshly baked Italian ciabatta bread. The smell of fresh bread transported me into another dimension. It reminded me of my childhood and of my parents, of Saturday afternoons when my mother used to bake bread so we could start the new week with fresh food on our table. I immersed myself in that sensory memory, a wonderful return to innocence. I was grateful for the moment, and I shared it with the owner of the shop. She smiled with gratitude: it felt good that someone appreciated her hard work and talent.

Starting the morning with an attitude of appreciation sets a positive tone for the rest of the day. So, wake up with gratitude. First thing in the morning, say, 'Thank you for this miracle of a new day.' Your inner light will shine more brightly, and the negativity of others can't affect it. This light becomes a source of inspiration and motivation to those around you, too. When you give away freely and generously, you will attract so much light that cannot be contained. It will overflow and radiate from your heart and soul, and this will leave those around you in a state of awe.

Do your best to stay positive. Commit to a blame-not, judge-not, complaint-free day. Complaining and pointing the finger only leads to unhappiness. Avoid blaming others and get rid of the victim mentality. This attitude allows you to take charge of your life in its entirety.

To help, you can use gratitude affirmations. Here are some that I use daily, but you can write your own. 'Every day in every way I am getting better and better.' 'I am grateful for discovering the source of power within myself, to create the life I desire and dream.' 'My life is filled with abundance and blessings, attracting perfect health and relationships.' These affirmations will activate your subconscious mind and your soul and connect with the Divine

Mind that underlies the whole of life and existence.

You could also create a written list of things, events and people you are grateful for and that you want to celebrate. Make the list as long as possible. For all these gifts, don't forget to say, 'Thank you, thank you, thank you.' Being grateful is saying yes to the subtle signals that the soul is sending to your mind. Almost anyone can develop the skill of listening to these whispered signals and to fine-tuning the inner ear to your heart's voice. How do we do it? With an attitude of gratitude overflowing from every thought, word and action.

When we pray, we usually hope that whatever we ask for will manifest quickly. We are seduced by short-term goals and programmed with limitations by our education systems, by popular culture and even by our parents. We are too obsessed with reaching our immediate goals, blinded by small desires, unaware of their perils. Unfortunately, we are not trained to be patient, but we must learn patience.

In life, there will be inevitable moments of

disappointment and discontent, and keeping a heart filled with contentment is no easy feat. A lack of patience can block the flow of positive energy. We expect things to be as we want them to be. We rebel when we are not getting exactly what we want or when we are not getting something fast enough. If only we realised that the universe is ready to give us a thousand times more than what we are capable of receiving. A wise person is grateful not only for the dreams granted today but also for those wishes denied yesterday. What if the universe had something better prepared for you all along?

Before we see any materialisation of our prayers, we have to purify our heart's intention. How do we achieve this cleansing? Through gratitude, and by not being afraid or too proud to ask for help. Anxiety and worries can poison and paralyse the soul, blocking the light from reaching our hearts. We cry for help only after we fail or when we are left with no other option. We selfishly think we can do everything on our own and that we don't need anyone else. That's not true. None of us is an island: we are all connected in a myriad different ways.

Many people are unable to move forward at this point and need a bit of help. This is where therapy and professional guidance can make a huge difference. I have seen many miracles and transformations in my hypnotherapy clinics. With guidance, and when the time is right, we all have great potential to change, to heal, to forgive. These are all small miracles. People often come back to me to share their new-found joy and happiness and to thank me. I remind them that the therapist's contribution is minimal, not more than 1 per cent. The rest is all due to their own belief in transformation and to the process of inner healing. The therapist is just a mirror reflecting back the possibilities to the client.

To know yourself is to learn about the divinity and the miracles in your own life. The heart opens to the beauty and the truth within. Think of it: you have already been granted so many things. Maybe you or your partner was cured of an illness. Maybe you were broke, and then things took an unexpected positive turn. Perhaps you managed, against all expectations, to build the house of your dreams. Have you shown any gratitude? How? And to whom? Remember, a loving heart is anchored in gratitude. Accept life with a smile and move on.

A focus on gratitude will give you wings and perspective. You will learn to build your life confidently with what you have available in the present moment and by not focusing on what is still beyond reach. Starting from this position, with a humble and grateful heart, you can handle anything, with a smile that wins in the end. You will understand that an arrogant and inflated ego is just a caricature of the materialistic world. A carefree heart filled with deep faith is anchored only in today.

Living in the present doesn't mean putting our head in the sand and ignoring the past. Most people are walking under the burden of yesterday's thoughts and problems. Sometimes, we need to face the past head-on, and that's a positive way to deal with problems.

The same goes if we project our thoughts and mind too much into the future, instead of living in the present. Anxiety increases when you fear that you will never accomplish your dreams. Gratitude attracts healing for you and everyone around. Whatever burden you carry, it will become lighter.

When you are in a state of gratitude, every day is a new beginning, without the burden of yesterday or tomorrow. Whatever worries trouble you, they will dissipate.

Gratitude opens our heart not only to others but also to ourselves. When you adopt the practice of gratitude, you share it. Your life is no longer just your own. Wherever you go, people will listen to what you have to say, and you, in turn, will listen to them, too. A grateful person has deep roots and feels unity with the whole universe. Nothing can disturb or cloud their mind and inner peace. If you meet someone like this, you could say they are living in a completely different dimension – one of peace and gratitude. Who would not want to achieve this state of mind?

It is important to stay grounded. The more successful you are, the more genuine and grateful you should become. When you are grateful, you create a new type of harmony between every living thing on the planet. The residues of your past are left in yesterday and they don't disturb your peace now.

It is an experience completely different from what you were conditioned to think: having limits that cannot be transcended. But with humility and a deep reverence for life, your heart can embrace the mind with love. The body has no other option than to follow the flow of love, energy and gratitude. You will reach a higher state of mind, and you will want this to last forever.

Gratitude is not just a thing to do. It's a process of becoming, of living in synchronicity with a higher purpose, an external manifestation. When you start the day focusing on the gifts of life instead of joining the sea of despair in the world, you become a magnet for positive things.

A grateful heart is a magnet for miracles. But what

you resist persists, and for this reason being grateful is not a destination; it is the journey itself. We are all creators of our own destiny, if we would only become more aware of the diamond mine hidden in our hearts.

Gratitude, faith and a resilient attitude are all simple ingredients that transform the ordinary into the extraordinary. These ingredients are available to any ordinary person, even to those with corrupted minds. What needs to happen next is accepting life from this perspective. This will lead to a purification of your consciousness and to a purity of thoughts.

Keep your heart open to whatever life throws at you. No matter what happens in your world, that diamond is safe because your real treasure lies within. So, do your best with what you have today. Be calm and serene, and with gratitude in your heart repeat again and again: *Thank you, thank you, thank you.* You can now expect miracles.

Remember

- Focus on what you are grateful for, not on what you think is missing.
- The only way to get rid of worries is to envelop yourself in an attitude of gratitude.
- Avoid blaming others and get rid of the victim mentality.
- Use affirmations daily.
- Create a written list of things, events or people you are grateful for.

Afterword

Beyond the diamond

My experiences bouncing back from the dark depths of depression taught me that a new life requires a new vision. Through the practice of visualisation, I was able to regain my strength and rebuild my confidence. A new habit for me, a bit like yoga for the mind, visualisation opened a window into my heart, and the more I focused on that window, and on the future, the stronger I became.

I started with a daily practice that lasted over two months – sixty-six days, uninterrupted. Before long, I felt stronger and started to feel a fire inside my heart: a good blaze, one that burned bright, fuelled my dreams and lit up the path in front of me. I shook off the shackles of old habits and the chains of a painful and traumatic past. Even physically, I felt a hunger for a radical transformation burning like a fire inside me. My priorities changed.

The purpose of visualisation is to gain mastery over our minds. Your brain is the organ inside your skull, but your mind is a sphere of energy. Although there's no instrument to measure it, you can feel its energy through your consciousness. The Russian inventor Semyon Kirlian captured the mind's energy in photographs, in the form of an aura around the head, and some people even have the ability to see auras with the naked eye. It's for this reason that you will see paintings of saints depicted as having an aura around their heads. The bigger and brighter the aura, the holier the person.

Wherever your consciousness wants to go, the energy of the mind follows. It is the energy of your mind and your consciousness that are connected to the Unified Field – to God, so to speak. You could even say that your consciousness is just another smaller piece of a bigger field; it is part of God's consciousness.

The mind has the distinction of being distracted by thousands of thoughts that arise every single second.

These thoughts have enormous power. Like radio waves, when you are in resonance with the frequency of your thoughts, your imagination starts to condense into something wonderful that will accelerate itself into existence. To reach that stage, the mind must be still and clear.

Visualisation can activate the tremendous creative power of imagination, which can make your dreams material – to manifest or materialise them. Solutions become clear the moment the heart embraces the mind. Through the daily practice of visualisation, you can guide your mind to tap into a deeper level of consciousness. You give yourself permission to dream with open eyes.

Often our dreams and visions are easily suppressed because of negative thoughts and the fear of the unknown. We listen too much to what other people have to say. They might even say we are not good enough to follow our own path. As a result, we ignore the voice that comes from inside us, and we miss out on extraordinary opportunities. So, stop listening to negative talk. What can you expect from a confused person? Only more confusion …

Through the simple but powerful practice of visualisation, we can mentally rehearse and create our dreams and plans, what we truly want in our lives. As if from thin air, we start to find solutions and answers to life's problems. Yesterday, the only things you could see were bollards and roadblocks; today, more options are available. Yesterday, you could only see a barren desert, an empty ground. Today, you see green shoots, and there is hope for a new season.

Everybody gets excited at the start of this process, but it is a practice that you have to continue for two full months. Don't stop halfway through. Go into the silence that envelops your heart and keep an attitude of gratitude every day. Bringing heart and mind together is difficult, but once we incorporate this practice into our daily habits, we gain more and more positive control over our lives. Bit by bit, you will rise again. You will start to climb the mountain of past conditioning. Before long, you will see the sun again.

This is because visualisation is sensing and believing in a bright future. It is like being attracted to light.

At first, I was vulnerable, open to a certain level of negativity and doubt. But the light and optimism coming from somewhere mysterious, deep inside, helped me to nurture the seed of a new vision in my mind.

When I realised what was happening, I tried to force this realisation onto others. This was wrong, and painful for everybody. It was like pushing against a wall, like swimming against a strong current. Eventually, I understood that I could change only myself. I had to become the change that I wanted to see in the world.

This realisation brought me great peace of mind. I finally understood that I was not born to fix everything that was wrong with this world. I could only change myself then hope that people around me would notice and follow my lead.

It was through becoming the best version of myself that I created a chain reaction in those around me.

Even then, their own transformations did not come through my influence or coercion but through them witnessing the great change flowing through me like a river, and seeing the joy and peace that were overflowing from my actions.

This time, I knew the change was going to last. I felt myself rising higher and higher, fuelled by a wonderful energy. This wasn't a fleeting glimpse of something greater outside myself. Something inside me was giving me wings. The combination of my visualisation practice and total faith loosened the grip of my old habits and allowed me to create a new beginning. It was like jumping out of a cold dark cave into bright light, stepping into a mysterious realm where everything was possible.

Once you wake up to the reality behind the veil of what you see, when you are awake spiritually, everything changes. I knew then that I had to move on to a higher conscious level, which I call 'visioning' – beyond visualisation. All the best writers, inventors and even businesspeople know that, with persistence, visualisation leads to visioning and that this new level engulfs their whole existence.

With advancements in technology, science and spirituality, we now understand that everything in this universe is connected. Those committed to the spiritual path, to self-exploration, try to decipher the timeless laws that govern the One Field, moving into a deeper level of awareness. Visioning goes beyond the limitations of the five senses. It is also the place where real healing begins. A deep sentiment of gratitude and thanksgiving takes over your mind, and you feel that your body has become a simple instrument.

What is the difference between visualisation and visioning? I've been asked that question many times, both by friends and by clients. It depends on the individual. If visualisation is seeing and believing, visioning is opening the window inside your heart towards yourself.

Once you embrace your life's positive purpose, you have to make sure that every thought, every word and every deed are in alignment with who you are.

At the end of each day, if you look in the mirror and know that you gave 100 per cent of yourself to your vision, to your dream, that there was nothing more you could do, that day was a success. The next day, start your routine again with the visioning exercise. Again, do your very best that day. One day soon, very soon, you will reach the destination you desire.

If you want your vision to persist and bear fruit, you have to think differently. When I was younger, before my experiences with depression, my satisfaction in life came from material wealth, from things I could hold and touch. It was a satisfaction that never lasted for long and that felt hollow and unfulfilling. It is not the mansion, the job or the fancy car that will make you happy. Now, I feel rich, but in a different way, with a different kind of wealth.

We are here on Earth to discover the beauty and the miracles of this life. The feeling of abundant overflowing comes not from outside, but from inside, from the heart. I discovered that the correct order of achieving anything worthwhile in life is (1) to be,

(2), to do, (3) to have. *Being* first, *doing* next, then *having* (as the very last step). Make sure you do not put *have* first, as most people do. I began to manifest this new abundance in my behaviour, and I grew in confidence.

Visioning means developing an intuition of the future, and it has a much clearer contour. There are four main signs, signals that you cannot miss: (1) The heart is your lighthouse. In the realm of visioning, the pure intention of the heart is everything, and, as a result, everything that is good and you believe to be true becomes true. (2) Fears and doubts are almost gone because you are operating with a heightened consciousness and a new belief system. (3) The vision has a very tight grip on you. It governs your mind. You drink, eat, breathe and love only through that vision. It's like the entire world is holding its breath, waiting for the realisation of your dream. (4) You sleep very little because the vision will not give you peace of mind until you reach your desired goal.

If visualisation is a linear path, visioning is a spiral staircase. Every time you pass the central point, you gather more wisdom and knowledge, and you discover new faces of the diamond hidden inside your heart. Sometimes, the intensity of your vision transforms the light of your diamond into a light as bright as the sun itself.

It is important to find someone to guide you in your vision, someone who has walked that path before you. They will ease the struggles and keep you pointed in the right direction. The journey is well worth the final discovery. Imagine your surprise when you realise that all this time, without knowing, you carried within the treasure you were looking for?

In the grand tapestry of life, the threads of who you really are intertwine almost invisibly with the limitations, roles and masks imposed by others and by society. By blindly accepting this, we lose our curiosity to find out why we are here, why we are alive. In our confusion and despair, happiness seems a very distant and unreachable concept.

You might think that everyone else is ahead of you, but this is not true. You only think this because your conditioning has already kicked in; you are comparing yourself with others. This is because you don't know yet what treasure is hidden inside your DNA. It's because you are searching in all the wrong places. Seeking treasure outside of yourself is a recipe for despair and disappointment.

You may be wondering, *What now? Where can I start?* Start from exactly where you are now. In this present moment, reading these words. This is the entry point into the mystery which is … yourself.

What about for once you stop chasing shadows of pleasures and just stop and listen to your heart. This is the first step of an inner journey towards knowing who is making yourself unhappy. Expect to be surprised! Because there is no God or gods doing it to you: You are creating it for yourself.

The silence flowing from the heart wants you to stop looking for pleasures and just experience the sweetness of joy instead. There's a big difference between chasing pleasure and experience joy. True joy comes from the soul, while pleasure is artificially implanted and created by others, who pass it along to you.

You were created for joy and not for pleasure, my travelling companion. You are more than the revolving thoughts of yours … and definitely more than those desires wanting to taste the drops of eternity. Accept the way you knew yourself till yesterday: with lights and shadows.

Asking a simple question like 'Who am I?' will ground you more and more. Synchronicity and spirituality have been weaving closer and closer, intertwining in a harmonious dance of hide and seek. Why be satisfied with coal, crumbs and broken dreams when you can enjoy the riches of the shining diamond nestling already in your heart?

You may ask yourself, 'Where can I begin?' There is no point in jumping agitated from one book to another. From one course to the next one. From one master to another teacher. It would be like mistaking the menu for the meal. Take everything from this book; learn and practise daily that which resonates with you. After a while, you will be surprised to start finding the answers within yourself, and you will become your own master. This is the part of the book's purpose: to guide you till the fog in front of you begins to clear. To taste the truth of yourself and life takes a true willingness, a dedication to daily practice.

I close these pages with the words of Japanese poet Matsuo Bashō: 'Do not seek to walk in the footsteps of the wise. Seek what they sought.'

You are ready.

By the same author